SHADOW LAND

OR

LIGHT

FROM THE OTHER SIDE

The spirits of the loved and the departed
Are with us, and they tell us of the sky
A rest for the bereaved and broken hearted
A house not made with hands, a home on high;
       Holy monitions — mysterious breath —
A whisper from the marble halls of death.
They have gone from us, and the grave is strong,
Yet in nights silent watches they are near;
Their voices linger round us, as the song
Of the sweet sky-lark lingers on the ear,
When floating upward, in the flush of even,
Its form is lost from earth, and swallowed up in heaven.

                               LONGFELLOW

Shadow Land

OR

Light

FROM THE OTHER SIDE

From the George Redway Edition of 1897

BY

Elizabeth d'Espérance

LOWOOD

Lowood Press: MMXI

From the George Redway Edition of 1897

Aksakof's references to page numbers in the introduction
have been changed to refer to the corresponding page
numbers in this edition.

Non-standard spellings have been preserved

To

HUMNUR STAFFORD

whose guiding—though unseen—hand and wise counsels, have here my mainstay and support on the voyage of life, and to those dear friends from the Great Beyond, and those who, standing by my side on Earth, have been my faithful helpers, co-workers, and fellow travellers on the journey through the shadows into the light, this book is dedicated with heartfelt gratitude and affection by

THE AUTHORESS.

PREFACE.

This book has been written at intervals during several years. I intended to hand over the manuscript to some one to publish after my death; but now having finished my work as a medium, I have come to the conclusion that I have no right to place on the shoulders of another, a burden of responsibility, that I would wish to escape bearing myself, and have decided that it is better to have the opportunity of defending the truths which I have here attempted to record rather than to leave the work to others.

A more weighty reason is the fact that suicides are increasing and I have never known a single instance of a sane man throwing his life away, when once he not only believed, but knew, the truths which have been part of my every day life since childhood.

Some months ago Stafford wrote an article on materialism which was reproduced in several German newspapers and a few weeks afterwards I received a letter from Baron X. saying, he had just lost a law suit which to him meant the loss of every thing. He had decided there was nothing left to live for and was arranging his affairs prior to taking leave of this world, when accidently the newspaper containing Staffords article came into his hands. He read it, wrote to thank the author and decided to give life another trial.

This circumstance encourages me to hope that, by making my experiences known, some others of my fellow-men may pause and consider whether earthly existence ends all and whether, in throwing away the great gift of life, they are not making a mistake which, a few moments after they would give worlds to have the terrible deed undone.

E. d'E.

———

INTRODUCTION.

To Mrs. E. D'espérance.

My Dear Friend!

You have had the kindness to send me the proof of your book, of which you ask my opinion. It is with pleasure that I comply with your request. The task you had undertaken was rather difficult, yet you have successfully achieved that at which you aimed. The danger to be avoided was that of saying *too much* or *too little*. In saying too much, you would have been entangled in particulars, as it would have required ten volumes, and more, to give a full record of your mediumship and yet, after all, it might have looked somewhat apological. In saying too little, you could remain obscure. You have however chosen a middle path, and, what is important, one gets a whole or complete impression—a very good one too. Perhaps even now you may remain obscure for others, but I speak for myself; as I have followed your mediumistic career in all its details for more than twenty years, I can understand you better than many others.

Endowed from birth with the fatal gift of sensitiveness, you, against your will, became a medium. Prompted purely by a feeling of duty towards truth, you did not refuse your help to those who were anxious to push further into the enquiry, in which you yourself became more and more interested. Soon you obtained very remarkable phenomena, and you were enraptured with the idea of having such palpable demonstrations of the glorious truth of immortality. What a consolation for poor, benighted humanity! What a new field for science! A missionary spirit inspired you and you were ready for any sacrifice for the triumph of the truth of spirit intercourse.

Long ago when I first became acquainted with spiritualism, I often thought that if I were a powerful medium, I would gladly give all my life, all my strength and means, for proving to all and everyone, the fact that there is a spirit world, and that communication with it is possible. Happily, I am not a medium, but you are, and you were animated by the same principles, as I had thought should have guided me, had I been endowed with the gift which is yours. In your life I see what the results would then have been in mine. Your career is a proof that, with the best intentions and the fullest sincerity, the results attained do not appear to be in proportion to the sacrifices we have made, or the hopes we have fostered. I can, therefore, be content with the idea that my fate would not have been better than yours. And why so? From ignorance of the phenomena, their laws and conditions. Because new truths cannot be enforced upon one's mind. Because the great pioneers of the cause are doomed to act alone, without finding help and counsel from others, who, to say the truth, are still just as ignorant as themselves. Truth is to be found in groping.

You began to be undeceived the very moment, when prompted by the "missionary spirit" you tried to give to the first comer, to every stranger, an actual demonstration (see page 114) of spiritual manifestation. It was then that you made a discovery "which seemed likely to upset all your plans for regenerating the world;" you observed that the manifestations, which were obtained so easily in your private circle did not take place before strangers, inasmuch as, they depended very much on the spiritual plane whereon they were enacted.

But your bitterest awakening began, when drawn unavoidably into the slippery path of materialisation, where all was then a mystery. To these experiments you had given yourself with a devotedness which was worthy of you. Sitting inside the cabinet but without being entranced, remaining perfectly conscious, what had you to fear? It was well that Yolande, whom you yourself have so often seen and touched, appeared outside the cabinet. What could be more convincing and tranquilising for you?

And, Lo! an unexpected accident precipitates you from heaven to earth!

You had the conviction of remaining in your place in possession of all your senses, and nevertheless your body was at the mercy of a foreign influence.

You fell a victim to the mysteries of suggestion. These mysteries were then almost completely ignored, and in the present case complicated by the question:—"From whom did the suggestion emanate?"

Appearances were all against you. You alone could know that your will had nothing to do with it and you were crushed by the mystery. It was very natural that for many years you could not even hear the name of spiritualism.

Ten years passed. I thought you were for ever lost to the cause. But time is the great healer, and some good friends induced you to sit again. A series of new experiments in photographing the materialised form were arranged. Splendid results, and another bitter awakening. Again you were accused when you knew you had done nothing else than sit for the benefit of others.

It was a repetition of the same mystery which you were incapable of solving, in consequence of the same ignorance.

It was at this juncture that I came to Gothenburg to again take up the experiments in photography. Having never submitted yourself to any tests used with the professional medium, you, however, allowed me to treat you as an impostor, submitting you to all the tests I could find necessary to apply. Never the least objection. I can testify that you were quite as much interested as myself in finding out the truth.

After a long series of experiments and much trouble, we arrived at two conclusions. The first was, that notwithstanding your full consciousness of remaining passive in the cabinet, your body, or a semblance of your body, could be used by a mysterious power outside the cabinet. Even your spirit friend Walter announced, through your own hand, that it might happen that nothing visible remained of you inside the cabinet. This was for you an exasperating revelation.

Another important point was gained—the doubts and suspicions of outsiders were to be excused, as they appeared to have more grounds than you ever thought it possible.

All this was most depressing.

Hence your resolution: "If I have any part in representing the spirit forms I must know it" (see page 206), and you decided that you would not sit behind the curtain again.

Under these new conditions you obtained most excellent results; and then took place a remarkable case, which you describe in Chapter XXIV "Shall I be Anna, or Anna be I?" I feared you would omit to mention this experience, but I am glad you have reproduced the details of it. The case is a precious one. You had there a palpable duplication of the human organism. This phenomenon lies at the root of all materialisation and has been the source of many, so called, exposures.

But for you, what a new perplexity!

I myself remember well the time, when laboring under the heaviest doubts, you were writing to me "Is all my life a mistake? Have I been misled? Have I been deceived and deceived others? How can I undo the wrong I have wrought?"

From the depths of that world, which was so near to you from your very birth and for which you have worked so earnestly and disinterestedly came the light for which you had prayed so eagerly—you received an answer to the doubts which were crushing you down. I am glad to see you again at the plough.

In your quite recent experiments in photography you succeeded in developing a new phase of your mediumship, which I have always supposed as belonging to you, but which at the time of my visit to Gothenburg, did not go further than the case reported at page 224. The recent results you obtained are completing your former experiments in materialisation and are in accordance with the beautiful vision which explained to you the mystery. We *cannot* see a spirit, but we *want* to see it. We cannot represent to ourselves a spirit otherwise than in a human form; and so "they" manufacture for that purpose what they can. Such were the forms and human heads, which you have seen and drawn in obscurity, (see page 95); such were, quite lately, the invisible human forms which you have photographed by day-light or with the magnesium light. I am inclined to suppose, that, if you had been sitting in the dark, you would have seen these forms also. Finally such were the materialised visible forms, which were photographed in Gothenburg and of which you give a specimen under the name of Leila at pages 183 and 185. All of these are only attempts to give us something tangible to our senses; attempts proving solely that behind these forms are spiri-tual agencies at work. That these forms were not to be taken for the images of spirits was told to us by them from the very begin-ning.

If you continue on these lines and become master of the con-ditions, one cannot tell where you may stop or what good results may be attained.

Such were my impressions, dear friend, when I was reading your book. It is a unique one. These are not the confessions of a recanting or apologising medium, but the open and sad story of the disappointments of a truth-loving and truth-searching soul, at the mercy of unknown but much promising powers.

Leaving this world of "shadows" I say unto you:—Go on! Go on! "Fais ce que tu dois, advienne qui pourra"—this is a good rule of yours. I shall not see your next achievements, but your mis-sion, I am sure, is far from being completed. Some day you will find your Crookes, who will understand the delicate nature of your mediumship, and how to cultivate and develop your mani-fold psychical gifts for the benefit of science and humanity.

Very truly yours
A. Aksakof.

Repiofka, Russia 5/17 September 1897.

CONTENTS.

———

		Page.
Dedication		7
Preface		9
Introduction		11

———

Chapter.

I.	The old house and its occupants	19
II.	My troubles begin	26
III.	Am I going mad?	35
IV.	A sunny holiday, and a shadow ship	38
V.	The mysterious essay	47
VI.	The fortune teller	55
VII.	My shadow people again, and table-rapping	61
VIII.	The table betrays secrets	66
IX.	Material passes through material	71
X.	Experiments in clairvoyance	77
XI.	Our spirit visitors	84
XII.	Science and spirit portraits	95
XIII.	A glimpse of truth	108
XIV.	Savants become spiritualists	112
XV.	Converts and converts	120
XVI.	New manifestations	128
XVII.	Materialised spirits	136
XVIII.	Yolande	145
XIX.	The Ixora Crocata	151
XX.	Numerous spirit visitants	164
XXI.	A bitter experience	174
XXII.	A fresh beginning	178
XXIII.	The Golden Lily—Yolande's last work	190
XXIV.	Shall I be "Anna" or "Anna" be I?	198
XXV.	From darkness to light	205
XXVI.	The mystery solved	214
XXVII.	Spirit Photographs?	223
XXVIII.	Investigators I have known	237

———

LIST OF ILLUSTRATIONS.

———

Portrait of E. d'E..Frontispiece

The "Shadow Lady".. 31

The "Shadow Ship".. 43

Walter.. 83

Humnur Stafford.. 88

Copy pencil sketch.. 97

    ”   ”   ”.. 98

Materialised Spirit..137

    ”   ”...138

Ixora Crocata..154

Photo of ferns... 157

    ”   ”   ”...158

Photos of plants.. 161

    ”   ”   ”.. 162

    ”   ” Strawberry.......................................163

Yolande...181

Leila...183

    ”.. 185

Golden Lily... 193

    ”   ”.. 195

Spirit Photo?..225

    ”   ”..226

    ”   ”..229

    ”   ”..230

    ”   ”..233

    ”   ”..234

    ”   ”..235

    ”   ”..236

———

SHADOW LAND

OR

LIGHT FROM THE OTHER SIDE.

———

CHAPTER II.

THE OLD HOUSE AND ITS OCCUPANTS.

All houses wherein men have lived and died
Are haunted houses, through the open doors
The harmless phantoms on their errands glide,
With feet that make no sound upon the floors.

We meet them at the doorway, on the stair,
Along the passages they come and go,
Impalpable impressions on the air,
A sense of something moving to and fro.

LONGFELLOW

WHEN one has made up one's mind to relate a story, I suppose it is the proper thing to begin at the beginning. I have therefore been trying to remember a fitting time or incident in my life to start from, but have given up the attempt because I cannot recollect any incident, in regard to which there was not something that led up to it and that would have therefore to be told as well. So I suppose I must go back all the way to where I began myself. This was shortly before the Crimean war, for my very earliest recollections are connected with my fathers home coming, and the rejoicings when peace was proclaimed. I could not understand what it all meant, but as it brought my father home it was to me a sufficient cause for rejoicing.

The experiences I have to relate, when looked on from the ordinary commonplace every-day life of this apparently work-a-day world, are strange and incomprehensible. Sometimes I have tried to put myself in other people's places, to see with their eyes, and judge with their understandings, and I have invariably come to the conclusion that they were not to blame for doubting the reality of the occurrences. For myself, these things have grown with my growth, and have been familiar to me from the beginning, since I can recall no time when they were not familiar and natural; so that the only curious thing to me seemed the fact that other people should not have the same experiences.

As a child I could not understand this fact; indeed the refusal of my companions to accept my version of what was going on around us sometimes irritated me beyond measure, and my frequent exhibitions of temper at their incredulity, gained for me the reputation of being "a little vixen" as well as "decidedly queer".

To my mind it was always the other people who were "queer"; and I thought it a great trial to have to listen to the wonder and incredulity, which frequently greeted my narration of something that to me seemed a trifling incident of every day life. However, as I grew older I began to understand that all were not gifted alike, and was magnanimous enough to make excuses for others in my mind on the plea that there was something lamentably wanting in them which prevented their seeing, hearing, or understanding so much that was going on around us, which was so plain and real to me. Child as I was, I naturally took upon myself to be their eyes and ears in much the same way as the companion of a blind man would do, till I met with so many rebuffs that I gave up the task, although pitying the infirmities of the ignorant grown up people who, half blind and half deaf, still persisted in rejecting my kind offices.

During my earliest childhood we lived in a gloomy old house situated at the east end of London,—a large house that had at one time been an imposing mansion; but that must have been centuries before, for now it was fast falling into decay and ruin. It was said either to have been built by, or resided in, by Oliver

Cromwell, I dont remember which; in any case it was very unlike modern residences. Large, ponderous, gloomy as it was, it had yet an air of superiority and dignity strangely out of place amid the newness of the houses which were springing up mushroom-fashion on all sides of it.

The house was doomed to come down, but its final destruction was deferred year after year, and meanwhile we lived in it.

Surrounding the ancient edifice was a courtyard in which one or two trees struggled for existence. It was paved by squares of black and white marble reminding one of a chequer board. The house was approached by a flight of marble steps that had once been beautiful but were now stained, worn, and broken. The door at the top of the steps was of ponderous carven oak, studded with iron bolts, and guarded on each side by great griffins which were the terror of my childish soul. Somebody had painted these monsters bright green, giving them red eyes and tongues.

The bolt-studded door gave admission to a gloomy oak-panelled hall, from which opened several disused empty rooms, also a broad staircase leading to the upper part of the house. Most of the rooms were oak-panelled and dark, the small windows never admitting light enough to make them cheerful, though at the back of the house—which looked out over a large piece of ground that had at one time been a garden, but was now only a grass-grown space—the rooms were of a more cheerful aspect, owing to the fact that the original small bottle-glass casements had been removed and French windows opening to the floor put in their places.

These latter were the rooms we lived in; the rest of the house was unoccupied and the rooms kept closed, except the lower part or kitchens, in which lived an old couple supposed to be caretakers.

How we came to live there I do not know, probably because the neighbourhood was convenient for my father, and perhaps also because, in spite of its gloomy age and its reputation of being haunted, the building was a more respectable and exclusive place of residence than the locality could otherwise boast.

The most gruesome stories were told of the ghosts who perambulated the many empty rooms, and my childish imagination was taxed to the utmost in picturing the doings of these strange visitants. I did not know what ghosts were supposed to be, but fancied they must be of the same ilk as the griffins at the great oaken door at the top of the steps, and was accordingly very much afraid of them.

At the same time I was very fond of wandering about from one empty room to another, and of sitting with my dolls on the broad low window seats, whence I would be fetched with an exclamation of horror and wonder by our servant, who considered my liking for the haunted rooms as "uncanny" and unnatural, threatening me with the ghosts and their vengeance if I persisted in invading their domains by myself.

I could never quite understand nurse's remarks about the loneliness of the rooms, though her threats about the ghosts frightened me. To me the rooms were never empty nor lonely;—strangers were constantly passing to and fro, from one room to another; some took no notice of me, some nodded and smiled as I held up my doll for their inspection. I did not know who the strangers were, but I grew to know them by sight, and look eagerly for them; I took my toys with me that I might show them, and a book of pictures that I prized above all the rest of my possessions.

Sometimes since I have wondered how it was that a little child should have been left so much alone to wander about the great house, with no other companion than a rag doll, but as my mother was an invalid and for a long time confined to her bed, I suppose there was sufficient occupation for our servant. There were no other children to keep me company; the little brother and sister who had been born only lived a few weeks, so that my earliest years were lonely ones, and I was left to do very much as I liked so long as I did not make my pinafores dirty—this being an almost unpardonable offence.

When my father, who was a sea captain, was at home the world changed for me; his presence was my very heaven; he was the one being that belonged entirely to me and of whose love I was sure. He was the only one who encouraged me to talk of my dreams and fancies, the only one who never scolded or spoke angrily to me; it was perfect happiness to sit on his knee and feel his arm around me, or to nestle at his side in the wide chimney corner and hold his hand while listening to the strange stories he told of foreign lands he had visited. Extraordinary stories they were, and, as I knew afterwards, sometimes invented on the spur of the moment simply to gratify my love of the strange and marvellous; but to me they were pure gospel because my father had related them.

After all they were not more wonderful than my dreams, though perhaps of a different character. It was nothing remarkable for me to hear stories of mermaids who lured the charmed seamen to the fairy palaces beneath the waves—nothing strange to learn of the wonderful music that only a few could hear. All this I thought I could understand, and it seemed to explain so much that was puzzling my small brain. It seemed to form a connecting link between myself and others. Somehow, child as I was, I had experienced a dull cold feeling of being in some way different from other people. I had heard myself designated as being "queer", and though in my own mind I had decided that it was the other people who were "queer", yet the consciousness of there being a something in which I differed from the rest caused me a nervous miserable dread of being misunderstood, and sometimes a passionate resentment against the intangible something which constituted the difference.

But these weird legends told me by my father had the effect of reconciling me, and even making me exult in being so well able to understand the mysterious people and sounds to which ordinary beings were blind and deaf. It was the same with me as with his heroes and heroines. I could see faces and forms where others saw nothing but mist. I could hear music and singing where others only heard the moaning of the wind. So I believed all he told me of nymphs, lorelies, watersprites, mermaids' enchantments, spells and the like, and the thought that some others were familiar with these things was the greatest comfort to me, and, as it were, reestablished me in my opinion of myself and of the "queerness" of those who did not see and hear the same things as I myself did.

As I grew older and was busy with lessons I had less time to dream in, less time to spend with my shadow friends, as I had learned to call them. Yet no sooner was I released from the monotony of the schoolroom than I joyfully took my way to the haunted rooms. My dreams came back, and imagination had full sway in peopling the old fashioned apartments and passages. I am now using the words "dreams" and "imagination" because other people used them and I do not know what other words to use, but they are not the right ones, since "dreams" and "imaginings" imply something fancied and unreal, but these particular "dreams" and "imaginings" of mine were very real, more real than any other part of my daily life.

To me the rooms were never dark nor empty. Sometimes on entering I would look round disappointedly at meeting no familiar form, then I would be startled at finding them suddenly peopled by strangers. Sometimes these shadowy figures were so real, so life-like that I mistook them for ordinary visitors. Scarcely ever did I go into a room without looking round for some possible shadowy occupant, and seldom did I look in vain. Some looked at me in a friendly, pleasant manner, and these I got quite accustomed to; others would take no notice, would pass me on the stairs or in the passages as though they never saw me. This vexed me sometimes and I felt indignant that my smile of greeting should pass unnoticed.

One of my shadow friends, was an elderly lady always dressed in black of some soft silken material that resembled satin yet was not satin. The frills of soft lace round her close-fitting white cap enclosed a sweet old face with smoothly banded grey hair. The cap was peculiar in shape having a high-standing crown while, at the back of the frills was passed a broad black band which came down under the chin and was tied there. Round her shoulders she wore a lace kerchief knotted at the breast.

This shadow lady seemed mostly to occupy one special room, though I saw her many times in others. The room was a rather long narrow one, low-ceiled and dark for the window was a small latticed one with diamond panes.

As our family grew bigger this room was oftener used, and as a consequence the old latticed window was replaced by a larger French casement with windows opening to the floor; the old-fashioned grate was also removed and a modern register stove occupied its place, but to my great delight the wide, deep recess on each side of the fireplace remained, for next to the window ledges behind the curtains, my favorite haunt was the chimney corner, where I could sit and pore over my book by the firelight, undisturbed and unnoticed.

After these alterations, the room newly furnished became a comfortable sitting-room, and, as it adjoined my mother's bed-room, was used by her as her special sanctum where she occupied herself with the family sewing.

Many times I wondered how my shadow lady would like this intrusion, for I rather resented any liberties that were taken with the rights of my shadow friends. It always seemed to me that they were the legitimate occupants of the unused rooms.

Somehow though I frequently spoke of these visionary in-habitants of our home I liked best to sit silently watching them; I was jealous of the thought of others sharing their acquaintance and friendship and exulted in the fact that I alone was privileged to know them.

CHAPTER II.

MY TROUBLES BEGIN.

Many were the fancies I had about these silent figures and many the stories I imagined relative to them. Many times I would wonder uneasily what it all meant and why others did not see them, but after having been punished for "romancing" when I related something of what I saw, I became chary of talking to any one about them. I did not like to be laughed at and still less to be accused of telling untruths.

About the time of the renovation of the room I have mentioned, a nurse girl related a series of ghost stories to me, in a manner which so frightened me that I dared not go into a room alone if it chanced to be dark, and even in daylight or moonlight I was terrified lest some uneasy ghost should be visible.

Night after night after listening with breathless interest to these blood-curdling stories I would lie with my head buried in the bedclothes, in a perfect agony of fear lest some visitant from the graveyard should make its presence known.

Yet, strange to say, I never once in my thoughts associated my shadow friends with the dreaded ghosts. They never inspired me with any fear. I could meet them at any time of day or night, return their friendly glance as they passed, or gaze curiously after them if they took no notice of me, I was even not afraid of the ghosts if I knew these friends were near me. I felt a sense of protection and safety in their presence, and never objected to be left alone in bed without a light when I was conscions that one or more of my shadow friends were in the room.

Many times in later years I have thought it was a strange thing that this apparently unnatural sort of existence did not arouse more curiosity or occasion more comment, but, as I have said, my mother's health was not good, and she was busily engaged in cares occasioned by the advent of babies in quick succession.

Meanwhile I was left very much to my own devices and though now a tall slip of a girl, was seldom required to assist in any duties except my daily lessons and perhaps at times some of the needlework of the family.

This last I was not particularly fond of, nor do I think I was fond of any kind of work except that of drawing, but for this I seldom had an opportunity, as my mother considered it a waste of time. I always had some sewing on hand, but there it generally remained till, impatient at its long delay, some one else finished it for me, scolding the while at my lazy habits. I bore the scoldings with perfect equanimity so long as I was left at leisure to pursue my favorite pastime, that of dreamily watching my shadow friends and speculating as to their histories.

At length one day, my mother annoyed at my dilatoriness, ordered me to sit in her room and sew a seam which appeared to me to be interminable. Work done by sewing machine was despised by mother, who had repeatedly declared she would not have such an abomination in the house. So the household sewing was a never ending work and, to my way of thinking, a hindrance to all rational employment. Not so to my mother, who seemed to find in it both a solace and a pleasure.

I took my seat beside the low work table where my mother sat and began my sewing. The room had a very different aspect now from that which it bore before the alterations had been made and I wondered what my shadow lady thought of it. As I glanced at the spot where I had been accustomed to see her I was both surprised and delighted to see the dear familiar figure in the corner by the chimney. She held something in her hands and her fingers moved rapidly; then I saw she was knitting. It was so long since I had seen any one knitting that my interest was at once aroused, and I watched the gleaming of the needles curiously, quite forgetful of the presence of my mother or the sewing on my lap.

"What are you looking at?" asked my mother sharply. "Can you not get on with your work?"

"Fancy, Mamma! The old lady is knitting stockings".

"What old lady?" began my mother, and then I found I had

made a mistake, for I saw the well-known tightening of the lips and frown on her brow as she continued: "Are you beginning again with that story? Have you not learned yet, old as you are, that such romancing as this is despicable and wicked? Have I not told you over and over again that I will not have it? You, a girl old enough to teach your brothers and set them a good example, instead of doing so are more trouble to me than all the rest put together. You are constantly in some tomboyish mischief or else dreaming away the time to the neglect of everything else, gazing into vacancy and hatching stories in order to frighten people. I thought as you grew older you would have dropped this absurd behaviour. I am thoroughly sick of wearying myself about you, for I don't know what is to be done to bring you to a sense of your abominable and wicked conduct".

I listened to this tirade with a miserably swelling heart, but at the same time I gave a surreptitious glance in the direction of my shadow lady wondering if she was a little sorry for me.

I felt very sorry for myself and very much injured. I had a wretched suspicion that there must be something wrong some-where in me. I had been told so often that I "romanced" and that I ought to be ashamed of telling things that were not true, but I had felt a kind of pity for the want of understanding in those who made such remarks. All the same I did not like to be suspected of being untruthful. I wanted to be good; I had tried my best and prayed till I was exhausted for help to become really good and not vex people so much—my mother in particular. Many times had I knelt beside my bed and prayed till I was overcome by sleep, that my dreams might leave me, or that I might not be tempted to speak of them. But alas! my efforts never availed me much.

Sometimes, especially when my father was at home or we had people staying with us, my shadow friends were invisible, and I forgot them for a while, there being always so much else to think about at such times. My father liked to have me with him and I rejoiced in his companionship. I had no companions of my own age, for I had been forbidden to associate with the girls who attended the same school. I never had had any playfellows except when my father was at home; then, it seems to me, the tomboyishness in my nature broke out and I became wild and excited over the games and fun which he encouraged.

As soon as he was gone and the house resumed the ordinary quiet monotony of everyday life my dreams came back; my shadow friends returned to their usual haunts and I welcomed them gladly. They were something that belonged to me and to me alone and I was secretly proud of having a world of my very own to which no one else had the *entrée*.

Sometimes in my pleasure and wonderment I felt that I must talk with someone about these strange people whom no one but myself seemed to see. My confidants were usually an old servant and my grandmother who came sometimes for a few weeks to stay with us. They always listened and commented. It seemed to me they were sympathetic, at least grandmamma was, for though she would tell me not to think or talk about such queer things and not to tell folks of my shadow people, yet she would many times relate such wonderful stories of the supernatural that I became thoroughly frightened and never at ease again till I had my shadow friends around me once more.

It never occurred to me that there was anything supernatural about them. I accepted their presence as a matter of course and was only nervous in their absence. I knew that no one saw them but myself, but had given up attempting to explain that fact and could only account for it on the ground that some people were "queer and dense".

That afternoon while I sat silently listening to my mother's remonstrances and complaints, with my eyes bent on the task I was doing, my thoughts were busy trying to reason out the cause and extent of my wickedness, for I really felt that I deserved many of the reproaches heaped upon me.

I was idle, I knew that. Lessons tired me, and I could not understand the words I learned by heart; I could not remember in the morning the lessons I had read at night; I could not work my sums correctly, and for these faults I was kept back in school. Grammar, geography, history, were so muddled together I scarcely knew one from the other. My writing was declared not fit to be seen, while as for sewing, which was my mother's strong point, I never took a needle in my hand but I would go wandering away into dreamland and only be brought to a sense of everyday life by a sharp reminder.

I thought of all these iniquities with a sigh, and felt that in some way or other I was a mistake. I wondered why I could not be like other girls. I could certainly get into mischief, climb, play ball, ride, run, jump and take part in the games, led by my father and young cousins, and could compete in most of the mischievous pranks perpetrated by them. It seemed to me I was a different creature at these times. Left to myself I lapsed into the dreamy idleness of old, and in a now busy household this was an unpardonable sin.

I felt all this and resolved that I would be different. I would study hard; I would no longer be put down in my class for badly written exercises and careless work; I would sew; I would help with the children; I would let them see I was good for something after all. As I made resolution after resolution of amendment, I felt myself growing quite good in anticipation of the marvel of obedience and industry I intended to become. I wondered if my shadow lady could hear and understand all this, and if she knew how I was being scolded.

I wondered who she was, if ever she had been a girl of fourteen and had had long seams to sew, and if she had been scolded for not doing them well. But it was knitting she was doing, wasn't it? Perhaps she never had sewing to do, but had to knit, knit, knit.

I glanced up at her; yes, there she was knitting, her fingers moving rapidly. I could see the needles flash under her swiftly moving fingers. I wondered at her cleverness, for her eyes were fixed not on her work but on me. Mother could not knit for I had heard her say so. I thought I would like to learn. It looked so pleasant and clever. I would ask grandmamma to teach me; I knew she could knit for I had seen her, but not so well by a long way as my dear shadow lady. I wondered if I could not learn from her, but no—she never began anything, and I must see how it began. Perhaps if grandmamma would put on the stitches for me I could manage, for then I could watch the shadow lady's

My "shadow Lady"
E. d. R

SHADOW LADY.

fingers and try to do the same—if only she would do it a little slower; grandmamma's fingers could not move so quickly if she tried ever so hard. I do not believe I could count quicker than she took off those loops—one, two, three, four, five; yes I could just keep time with her. Why how soon one could knit all the stockings required for the family. Mother would not be able to say I was idle then.

A sharp voice disturbed my calculations. "Why are you not sewing? It's no use me speaking, you are certainly enough to try the patience of a saint. You pay no attention to what I say, but do your very utmost to annoy and aggravate me. What are you looking at? What is there in the corner?"

My mothers querulous tones brought me back to a sense of my wrongdoing.

"It is only the old lady knitting", I explained, "and"—

"Silence, you wicked girl. Never mention such things to me again. I hear enough of your falsehoods from others. How dare you repeat them to me? Take up your work."

I had let it fall in my fright when her voice aroused me from dreaming.

"Let me see you lift your eyes from that seam till it is finished, or glance in that direction again, and I will box your ears thoroughly and see if that will help you to remember."

She was now really angry, and I tremblingly took up my work and resumed my sewing in silence.

O mother Eve! had you known what a legacy you were leaving to your daughters, I wonder if the knowledge would not have stayed your hand from the forbidden fruit. What unconquerable longings have we not inherited, to do that one thing we have been forbidden to do! I did not want to raise my eyes from my work, I really wanted to do as I was told, but somehow the temptation to see how the knitting was progressing, and whether the lady understood the state of affairs between my mother and me, was too strong and I looked over to where she was, looked and suffered the threatened punishment, for a stinging box on the ear brought me to a sense of my disobedience.

I knew I deserved it, but that did not mend matters, and I cried and sobbed bitterly, nor could I restrain myself when the door was opened and the doctor who was in attendance on my mother at the time entered the room.

I rushed out when he came in and seated myself on the stairs, and, covering my face with my hands, wept in my grief and shame.

After a while the door was opened and I was called in. Choking back the tears, I entered the room. My mother still sat in her easy chair looking disturbed and angry. The doctor was walking the floor. As I came in he sat down and taking me by the hand, patted it in a friendly manner and said kindly:—

"I am sorry to see you crying, but you know your Mamma is not well and you should try to please her instead of vexing her so much. Tell me what all this story is about, that you see things other people do not see, old women knitting and such like. What is it all about? Tell me."

He looked kindly and sympathisingly at me, patted my hands, wiped the tears from my eyes and urged me to talk.

Thus encouraged I told him of what they called my fancies or my dreams, but which were no dreams or fancies but realities. I told him of the shadow people who were our everyday guests; of the old lady who worked so industriously and who looked so kindly at me, of her knitting, her cleverness; of the finely dressed gentleman with long curling hair and the feathers in his hat and the sword by his side, and the large spurs on his heels; of the man with a frilled collar which stood up round his neck, making him look as though his head rested on a plate; of the ladies with silken dresses and white hair, their frills and furbelows, their curious manners—I told him all; and of my troubles at not being believed and how dreadful it was to be suspected of falsehood.

"But its true", I said, "every word; they are there and I do see them. I don't tell falsehoods."

"Yes", said the doctor, "I believe you, I don't think you mean to tell untruths."

Oh! how my heart bounded at these words and went out to the man who believed me.

"Yes, I believe you see these things that other people do not see, I have known of others who have done the same, who have seen men and women and animals which did not really exist. *But these people were mad.* They persisted that they saw shadows moving about them, that they saw old men or women waiting about in corners. They have gone on seeing, first one thing, and then another, till they have become dangerous and we have had to send them to a lunatic asylum to be taken care of."

It seemed to me that his words froze the blood in my veins. I could only stare at him in horrified silence. Was this then the meaning of it all? Was this the secret of the beautiful dream world in which I had spent so many happy hours? Were my shadow friends not there? Did they not exist? Was every one right when they said they were not there, and only I wrong?

I saw them—in that I was not mistaken—but if they did not exist and I saw something which had no existence, it was clear there was something wrong. I had never thought of the matter like this before, but now—horrible thought—I must be growing mad.

All that day and night I suffered torments. To be mad—what did it mean to be mad? I thought of all the dreadful things I had heard, of crimes committed by maniacs, of the horrors of mad houses, of padded rooms, irons, strait-waistcoats; and I shivered with fear, and prayed almost frantically that I might be kept from going mad.

CHAPTER III.

AM I GOING MAD?

My soul its secret hath, My life its mystery
Hopeless the evil is, I have not told its history.

LONGFELLOW

THE more I reflected, the more I became convinced that the doctor was right, and the horror and fear nearly deprived me of my senses.

Though nearly fourteen years of age I was singularly childish in many ways. Brought up, as I had been, almost isolated from other children outside of the family circle, and seldom admitted to the society of the elder members of the family, I had grown up very ignorant of many things with which girls of the same age are perfectly conversant, and in this trouble I had no one to help or advise me. My father was away, and my grandmother, who was always kind, was in her own home or making her usual long periodical visit to some one of her children.

Our old nurse was there, but somehow I disliked to confide in her, for if I were really mad, then the fewer who knew it the better, and I must talk to no one of the illusions to which I was a victim.

I wondered if madness could be cured by medicine, and if the doctor could not do something to help me. Perhaps it was only something wrong with my eyes, for I remembered with a pang that whenever I had voluntarily or involuntarily put out my hand to touch the shadow people when passing me, my hand had not come in contact with anything although I had remarked that they shrank from my touch. From this circumstance I had called them "shadow people", but hitherto I had not thought much about it. Thinking over it now, I wondered if it were not my eyes which played me false. This idea was a much pleasanter one than that I was mad, but the fear haunted me nevertheless night and day. I remembered a servant telling me that one of the practices in mad houses was that of tickling the soles of patients feet; she had read it in a book called "Valentine Vox", she said, and knew it was true. I could not bear to have my feet tickled, I knew that; but perhaps it would not make me laugh so much if they kept it up very long. I wondered if mad people lived very long. I was afraid they did, for I remembered an old, old man who sometimes went about the neighbourhood selling clothes pegs or begging; I remembered his stopping our servant one day and frightening her with terrible oaths and curses. He was mad, she said. I wondered if I should ever be like him and learn to swear or go about with unwashed face and unbrushed hair. Much better to be locked up in a mad house than that.

All the horrors of mad houses that I had ever heard of passed through my mind before I slept that night after the interview with the doctor, and I resolved that as long as was possible I would hide my real condition from everyone. If I were mad then no one should know it and perhaps after all it was a curable malady for it was not always that I was so afflicted. Occasionally, months at a time, the shadows would vanish and only return when I was alone and indisposed for work or study; then I welcomed them with rejoicing.

After this time everything was changed; my pleasure, in seeing the shadowy forms flit by me or meet me on the stairs and passages gave place to a sinking feeling of desolation and fear. I had no cause for pleasure now in the sight of the familiar forms, for were they not so many evidences that my disease was not leaving me?

Presently another idea came to me. It was Satan who caused my eyes to see things which did not exist. This threw a new light on the subject and I was almost glad, for anything was better than being mad. If it were Satan, then God could help me, and I knew He would,

After this a glimpse of a shadow, whether real or imaginary, sent me to my bedroom and on my knees to pray. Many times, morning, noon, or night, I was driven to my knees to implore deliverance from the machinations of the evil one.

I became shy, timid, and nervous,—afraid to move from one room to another; afraid to remain alone at any time day or night, watchful of my every word lest I should betray my madness; afraid lest anyone should notice that I turned my eyes in any direction but that in which I was going, for fear they should suppose I saw the "shadow people". I became eager for occupation, and afraid of being without work of some kind, because I had learned the hymn wherein we were told that Satan finds mischief for idle hands.

The Bible became my constant companion, either carried in my pocket by day or clasped to my breast at night. With this I fancied I was armed against the powers of evil.

How long this state of things lasted I do not quite remember, though it seems to me I grew years older in the months that elapsed before my fathers next home-coming.

He was a little disturbed at my pale face and want of flesh and questioned me as to my scared nervous manner.

"She is growing", said mamma; "all girls get pale and thin when they grow as fast as she is doing".

"I would rather she did not grow if it makes her look so pale and delicate", said my father. "She should be out more, and not kept poring over those stupid books and sewing. We must see if she cannot have some change that will put a little color in those pale cheeks".

After many plans had been proposed, discussed, and rejected, it was ultimately decided that, in default of anything better, I should accompany my father on his vessel during a cruise in the Mediterranean, which cruise he expected to last two or three months.

———————

CHAPTER IV.

A SUNNY HOLIDAY AND A SHADOW SHIP.

> There is a spectre ship, quoth he,
> A ship of the dead that sails the sea,
> And is called the Carmilhan.
> A ghostly ship, with a ghostly crew
> In tempests she appears
> And before the gale, or against the gale,
> She sails without a rag of sail,
> Without a helmsman steers.
>
> Longfellow

THIS holiday was without exception the happiest time of my life. Everything was new, fresh and delightful. The great vessel itself was a source of never failing interest. My father's love of animals, restricted at home, here had full sway and one part of the vessel was quite a little menagerie. Fowls, geese, pigs and a couple of goats occupied their respective pens. The goats had been brought for the purpose of supplying me with milk, which, however, I disliked; but they provided me with considerable amusement, particularly at milking time, when they seemed to find their greatest delight in evading the attempts of the boy to milk them.

The sky-lights of the saloon were filled with choice flowering plants and among them hung cages of singing birds. The most remarkable member of the menagerie was, however, a black monkey whose mischievous pranks were at once the torment and delight of every creature on the vessel. It was extravagantly fond of my father, but for some cause or other it never took kindly to me. Father said it was jealous. Perhaps it was, for we noticed many times that if my father caressed me, the little creature would go away to its cushion in the corner and sit looking sad and melancholy, nor would it leave its place so long as I remained beside him.

Last, but not least, was Jack, an immense Newfoundland dog, who was an old acquaintance and who from my coming on board the vessel seemed to constitute himself my inseparable companion and protector.

I soon became acquainted with all on board, both officers and men, and with so many companions and play-fellows, so many new interests, new friends, new scenes, and the never ceasing newness of sea and sky, the whole of this sunny holiday became—as I called it then and since—simply "heavenly".

One of my particular friends on board was the chief officer, Lieutenant N—. Although chief officer he was the youngest among them; though, to my childish ideas of age, anyone above twenty seemed well on in years. It was he who superintended the daily lessons which my father, in deference to my mother's wishes had undertaken to see religiously carried out, therefore insisted upon.

But father's weak point—or greatest virtue, as it seemed to me—was clemency, and a few coaxing words or a kiss would generally buy off an hour's study. As I gained in health I proved a refractory pupil. It was impossible to study when the sun was shining, or the birds twittering, or the dog and monkey were heard gambolling overhead. As I closed my books, my father would shake his head, and say, "Well, just this once but no more". Lieutenant N. then undertook my education, and between the two I managed to do pretty much as I pleased. The only item of knowledge which I remember to have acquired was to "Box the compass" which I did many times to the delight of my new friends, who admired my proficiency in gabbling over the degrees from North to South and from South back to North again.

Certainly I learned many things with respect to the places we visited. The history of the Italian towns, modes, manners and customs of the people, the discoveries and excavations of Pompeii were taught me in a manner which impressed themselves on my mind as no amount of reading could have done.

In short it was a perfectly enjoyable education. My dreams and strange fancies left me. My shadow friends were forgotten. My sleepwalking to which I had been addicted was cured, and I was, like other girls of my age, healthy, happy, full of mischievous fun and tomboyish tricks, disliking confinement and restriction, and delighting in little adventures, especially if a spice of danger were connected with them. In these I was aided and abetted by the Lieutenant, who was constantly planning fresh diversion while at sea or arranging excursions when in harbour.

My father allowed me to do pretty much as I liked, though he sometimes pretended to look dubiously on some of the proposals, and wonder what mamma would say, if she knew. Still he was delighted at my improved health and spirits and would frequently remark that no one would know me when we returned home. He usually accompanied me on my shopping expeditions and supplied me with money for my numerous purchases, so that I felt like a millionaire when at last we were recalled to England, and I surveyed the amount of property I had accumulated during the three months we had cruised about among the quaint towns of the Italian coast. My possessions, I found, included slippers, gloves, eau de cologne, corals, shells and marble ornaments, vases, paperweights of mosaic work, needle cases, and scent bottles of lava.—The consideration of how to dispose of these treasures among my friends at home gave me great pleasure and exercised my thoughts very fully for many a day. Then occured an incident so strange and incomprehensible that it cast a shadow over this happy holiday and brought back to me the sense of my former everyday life and its trouble which I had almost forgotten.

The day had been intensely warm, so that the breeze caused by the swift progress of the steamer was extremely refreshing. The sun was setting in a bed of fire. The sky was wonderful in its beauty of colour,—crimson, gold, yellow and opal. The sea was smooth and still, not a ripple to be seen except in our wake, where the curling white foam reflected the beauty of the colours above it, making one of the loveliest scenes on earth.

Lieutenant N. was on the bridge, and I, as usual stood beside him, eagerly discussing the events of the past few days, the scenes we had passed through, the merits or demerits of the purchases made on our last excursion on shore. My tongue was, as my father often put it, "running nineteen to the dozen". We had during our conversation remarked several vessels in the distance and the subject of the purchases having been discussed and dismissed, I turned my attention to the ships, anxious to show my ability to distinguish one class of ship from another, and classify them sailor fashion. Lieutenant N. and I did not agree as to whether a vessel outlined against the skyline was schooner or brig, I persisting that it was the one and he the other.

"Take my glasses and you will see I am right", he suggested, offering me his telescope.

I turned to exchange glasses with him when I was almost petrified by seeing a large vessel close before the bows of our own. We had been looking aft during our conversation, and, intent on our argument, had not noticed for a few minutes what was going on forwards.

"Look, look!" I cried fearfully.

"What at?" asked my companion.

"At the ship! Won't you stop? We are going to meet—Stop, stop! Why don't you stop?" I gasped in terror, for the vessel was so close that the men on her deck could be clearly distinguished, and we were nearing each other with frightful rapidity.

"What ails you, child? What ship? What do you mean? Why should we stop?"

I grasped his arm and turned him round, for he was looking at me in surprise, not at the vessel we were swiftly approaching.

"Now can you not see?" I screamed.

"Are you blind?" And in my fright I shook him, repeating "The ship! the ship! stop! stop! stop!"

He took no notice of what I said, but loosened himself from my frantic clutch and drew me down on a seat that had been placed for me in a sheltered corner. My only idea however, being that we were going headlong to destruction and that I must be with my father, I struggled from his grasp and was rushing from the bridge when he caught and held me, insisting that I should be still.

"How can I be still when you are going to drown us all? Let me go. Father! Father!" I moaned, struggling anew.

Then I cowered down and hid my face against his arm, for the strange ship was now looming full over our bows, her white sails gleaming rosy red in the light of the setting sun. One man on her deck was leaning with folded arms against the bullwarks watching the on-coming of our vessel. All this I saw in the brief glance I gave before hiding my face. Everything turned black before me, my heart stood still while I waited for the inevitable crash. Oh, the agony of those moments! No lapse of time will efface from my memory the thoughts that rushed through my brain while waiting for the meeting of the two vessels. It seemed to me that a life-time was crowded into that second.

"What is the matter, why are you so afraid?" said Lieutenant N. putting his other arm round my shoulders. But I could not answer, I could only moan and tremble.

The crash was long in coming. I ventured at last to raise my eyes. *The vessel had disappeared!* The relief was so great that a sob almost choked me, and the tears began to stream down my cheeks. "Where is it? Which way did it go?" I stammered when I could get out the words.

"I don't know what you are talking about", replied the Lieutenant. "There has been no ship near us. Do you think I should not have seen it had there been one?"

I stood up and glanced uneasily round. There in our wake was the vessel with her sails fully set. I saw each rope of the rigging and noticed that the sails, this time between the setting sun and me, were not rosy red as before, when the red glow lay full on them, but grey. I saw the men moving about on the deck. I saw the pennant flying at the mast head. The vessel did not seem to be fifty feet from us, but the distance was rapidly increasing. It was quite clear to me that we had in some way *passed through each other* and were now speeding on our different ways.

"Can you not see it now?" I asked, pointing to the receding ship.

"I can see nothing", replied he shortly.

The sharpness of his tone and the reaction of the intense

The "Shadow Ship".

excitement I had undergone were too much for me and I gave way to tears and sobs, refusing to be comforted in spite of all the soothing words of my friend. I felt horribly tired and trembling. The tears would fall, although I tried to subdue them, till at last Lieutenant N. suggested that I should go to my state-room and rest, adding "But don't awaken your papa, and don't tell him what frightened you or what you saw".

I nodded my head and went slowly down to my cabin. I wished he had not told me not to awaken papa and not to tell him, for it would have soothed and comforted me to have told him all.

I paused at his door, listening for some sign of his being awake, for I think in spite of all I should have gone to him, but there was no sound except of deep breathing; so I went to my little state-room and crept into bed, crying myself miserably to sleep.

My waking thoughts next morning were of the mysterious vessel and the strange behaviour of Lieutenant N. My first impulse was to rush to my father and tell him all about it; so I hastened to dress in order to catch him before he went to the breakfast table. While brushing my hair and thinking it all over it struck me as very curious that Lieutenant N. wished me not to tell my father. Then it flashed on me that it was because my father would blame him in some way for going so close to the strange vessel. Although no damage had been done, I knew that for a steamer to come into such near proximity to a sailing vessel was a breach of the rules of the road. I had been told that a steamer must always make way for a sailing ship, or in sailor parlance "give her a wide berth" on the open sea, and knew that in allowing his vessel to come so close to the other Lieutemant N. had committed a breach of the law which would make my father very angry.

I remembered, too, that I had been cautioned many times about chattering to the officer in charge, while he was very busy or engaged in directing the course of the steamer, and I could not help admitting to myself that I had been chattering to him hard enough just then. So this then was why my father must not be told. I began to understand that something both unpleasant and serious might result to Lieutenant N. did my father learn of the catastrophe we had so narrowly escaped. I mentally resolved that I at least would not get my friend into trouble. With this resolution I seemed to put an uncomfortable burden on my shoulders, but I was glad to bear it for my friend's sake. All that day, though we met, walked and talked together as usual, the occurrence of the previous evening was not mentioned.

The following day at dinner, my father asked me why I had cried the other evening because I had fancied I saw a ship. This way of putting it caused the indignant blood to mount to my face and tingle to my very finger tips. I knew not what to say, till an amused laugh from Lieutenant N. and the smiles of the others at the table, told me that the affair was no secret. This was too much for me and my resolution, and I rapidly poured forth the whole of the story. I spoke quickly and passionately, the whole terror of the scene coming back as I related it.

"Tell me quietly", said my father, when I had finished with a sob.

I repeated the story.

"Why did you not tell me when you came below?"

"Lieutenant N. said I might not awaken you. I wanted to tell you yesterday, and was going to do so, but I thought you would be angry with him for going so near the ship, and thought that was why he didn't wish me to tell you. So I didn't and I'm sorry I've told you now, only he laughed at me", I concluded resentfully.

After this my father left me and went to talk with the officers on deck. I heard no more of the matter till later in the day when he came to me and told me, in a vexed tone, that I must never make such an upset or say such things as these again. He had, he said, made very careful enquiry of the men on watch as to the vessel, which I declared I had seen, but they all maintained that no such vessel had passed near us since leaving port nor had they noticed anything except that I was crying bitterly. Thus the whole matter was shrouded in mystery, and I saw plainly that I must not expect to be believed in the face of so much evidence to the contrary.

The old weight of anxiety and dread that had lifted itself from my heart during the long holiday seemed to again settle down upon me. I began to wonder and speculate as to the possibility of there being shadow ships as well as shadow people. In short the old trouble came back and made me heavy-hearted and wretched, though the various little excitements incident to the life on board ship prevented me taking it so seriously as I had done previously.

After this my holiday was spoiled. A something had arisen between my father and me,—a cloud, slight it is true, yet it formed an intangible barrier to our pleasant relationship. He thought me guilty of falsehood, and I was miserable and indignant at being under suspicion.

Nor could I disabuse my mind entirely from the idea that Lieutenant N. desired to screen his non-observation of the vessel by persisting that it had never been there. I was also indignant with him for mentioning the matter after he had forbidden me to do so. A long time after this I asked him why he had told me not to tell papa and he replied,—"Because you were in such a state of agitation and excitement, that I thought it would not be good if your father scolded you for having such silly fancies— that was all".

However my holiday was spoiled, and I began to long for the end of our voyage.

———————

CHAPTER V.

THE MYSTERIOUS ESSAY.

"In the same hour came forth fingers of a man's hand, and wrote over against the candlestick upon the plaster of the wall of the king's palace; and the king saw the part of the hand that wrote".

DANIEL Chap. V VERSE 5

DURING the next year or two, which I spent at school, I was to a great extent free from both dreams and shadows. My education had been greatly neglected, and in order to make up for this I was obliged to work rather hard. I had been placed in a class of girls much younger than myself, and even here I found myself more ignorant of the ordinary rudiments of education than my class-mates, but in less than a year I had worked myself up till I was allowed to read many subjects with the girls in the highest classes.

My health was good, my work was a pleasure, and I pursued it eagerly. Fun and frolic, too, among girls of my own age were delightful experiences from their very newness and soon no game was complete without me. This spirit of fun had some disadvantages, for after a while I was generally credited with being the ringleader in any mischief that might be discovered; but, this notwithstanding, I enjoyed my studies and liked my teachers.

The last term which I attended happened also to be the last term for several of the older pupils. At the end of it an examination of more than usual importance was to be held, and both teachers and pupils seemed desirous of doing credit to themselves.

For some weeks previous to the first of June our amusements had been laid aside and our usual noisy sitting-room had been transformed into a quiet study, where we sat, after the day's work was over, busied with the preparation of such special tasks as would have a telling effect at the semi-public examination.

My own work was to a great extent complete, with the exception of an essay which I was expected to write. My attempts in that line hitherto had been ignominious failures; in fact such essays as had been sent in under my signature owed rather more to the help of a classmate than to my unaided efforts. It was an open secret in our class that Lydia Olive's translations and my essays ought in reality to have borne reversed signatures. This time it had been announced in a severe tone, specially directed to us two, that these essays must be absolutely and entirely original, and that no one was to offer, or accept, help in their composition.

If I remember rightly, the subject selected for me was "Nature" or "What is nature?" As one week after another brought the end of the term nearer, I was many times in despair because of my inability to put together a dozen lines on the subject. Many times I began, "Nature is the Mother of us all" or "Nature comprises all that is in the Universe", and just as many times I stopped. Not another sentence could I find that did not seem crude, disjointed, or even absurd. Sheet after sheet of paper I destroyed and made an elaborate beginning on another, only to end in the same manner. Every evening as I put away the writing materials I wondered what would become of me if the next day brought no better result. Every night I went to bed with the determination not to go to sleep but to think it out and commit the result of my thinking to paper first thing in the morning, but alas! after putting my head on my pillow my resolutions were of no avail, and I was no nearer the completion of my task.

The days seemed to fly. The girls were now busily employed in carefully recopying their pencilled notes. I looked miserably on at the progress of the copper-plate-like writing; I saw the elaborate signature and the complacent smiles with which each girl regarded the document before her. But it was of no use; the more I tried the more stupid I became. I could only cry in secret over my trouble.

Many times I shut myself in the bedroom and on my knees prayed that I might have some ideas given to me, but praying seemed of no use, my head was as empty as ever.

"Nature is the mother of us all", began to ring in my ears and dance before my eyes. The words seemed to chase each other in my empty head, playing at leap frog, jumping and dodging each other till I sometimes laughed aloud at the thought.

It wanted only three or four days to the great day. All our drawings, papers, and hand-work had been collected and the essays had been sent in. When asked for mine I falteringly explained that it was not ready. I was told that I had very little time left and it must be prepared without further delay.

That night I provided myself with a candle, paper, and pencils, and after we had retired I sat up in bed determined to accomplish something. I had written those dreadful words again when some grumbling voices told me to put out the light or their owners would do it for me. There was no alternative but to obey. I could only turn my face to the wall and cry till I fell asleep, resolving to wake early, as soon as it was light, and write something no matter what. Next morning, however, I did not awake till some one threw a wet sponge at me, when I was aroused to a miserable consciousness of my inability to keep to my resolutions.

My first glance was at the sheets of paper and pencils lying unused on the table beside my bed; they were strewn in disorder, some on the floor. Stooping with a heavy heart and head to gather them up, I saw that most of them were covered with writing. My first thought was naturally that I had by mistake brought written sheets instead of clean ones to my room the night before, but a second glance shewed me that the writing was my own. Puzzled and bewildered I sat on the bed-side in my night gown, unheeding the raillery of my companions who were dressing and making fun of my laziness, or studious mood, as they called it by turns. But I was absorbed in the writing and did not notice them. Page after page I read eagerly, astonished and delighted.

I did not know how the writing had come there, and at first I did not think about it at all, only of the pleasure I had in reading the beautiful thoughts, expressed in the neatly turned poetical sentences. "Look here, girls", I said; "listen to this", and I began to read aloud:—"In the beginning God created the heaven and the earth, and the earth brought forth grass and herb yielding seed after its kind and the tree yielding fruit whose seed was in itself after his kind, and God saw that it was good."

"Oh, stop, stop", they exclaimed; but I went on page after page in which was unfolded as in a picture the vision of the new world opening up its first glorious beauty under the new Sun, new Moon, new Stars, each fresh development more rich in beauty and wonder than the last; from the circling stars pursuing their appointed course to the tiny blade of grass absorbing its rich colour from the rays of sunlight.

So eagerly did I read that I did not notice that my hearers were far from feeling the same rapturous delight as myself, and not till I reached the end was I conscious of the sneering remarks and expressions of opinion as to my pretended inability to write an essay.

It was with curious feelings I entered the schoolroom that morning, I scarcely noticed the coolness and ill-humour of my class-mates, for my head was filled with pictures which the mysterious writing had called up. I felt restless and excited, impatient till the half hour's recess gave me an opportunity of re-reading it. It was not till then that the strangeness of the whole thing struck me.

"How had it come?" "Who had written it?" "When had it been written?" Then the thought that someone was playing a trick on me made me half frightened; but no, it was in my own handwriting, this was unmistakable. No one could dispute that fact. I must have written it, but when? In my sleep? I had heard of such things, but the thoughts were not mine. I had a miserable feeling that I was utterly incapable of putting together half a dozen sentences, let alone these beautifully rounded periods,— so poetical, yet so strong, that in reading them one was carried away on wings of fancy to the scene of Nature's birthplace.

All that day I was tormented by self-inflicted arguments for and against claiming the ownership of the writings, and hurt by the innuendoes of my companions, that my inability to write an essay had only been a pretence or ruse to get them to send in their work and then come in last with mine with which I intended to utterly eclipse them.

More than once I decided not to use it, but the temptation was very great.

The matter soon reached the ears of our head mistress and I was requested to bring the papers to her private room, which I did in fear and trembling. Telling me to be seated, she took the sheets of paper and glanced rapidly over the first page, then, looking at me with the coldly severe countenance with which she usually regarded delinquents, she said:—"Where did you get this? Have you copied it from any book?"

"No Ma'am".

"Be good enough to explain", she continued.

I then told her timidly how I had failed in all my attempts to write an essay on the subject chosen for me, and of my distress in consequence; how I usually took pencil and paper to my room at night in readiness to write anything I could think of after I went to bed, because it seemed easier to think when one was lying down; but how I always went to sleep and never had any thoughts that I could remember next morning. I told her how on the last night I had prayed for thoughts, and tried to write in bed, but had been obliged by the grumbling of the other girls to put out the light and I had lain down and wept till I fell asleep; then how I had found the papers covered with writing next morning when I awakened.

"Then who do you suppose wrote it?" asked Madame.

I answered that I could only suppose I had done it myself, since the writing was my own and the two pencils were used quite down into the wood, showing that they had done service.

"But you have no recollection of writing it?"

"No."

"Then do you consider it honest to pass it as your own?"

This was the question that was troubling me and I tremblingly said:—"I don't know what to do; I want somebody to tell me what is right; it makes me so unhappy not to know."

And the tears, never very far off, were now falling down my cheeks. I think my evident distress must have softened her opinion of me for she answered quite kindly, "I will read it through and think the matter over, and then tell you what I think is your duty." So I left the room with a lightened heart glad to have shifted the responsibility on to the shoulders of another and a wiser person than myself.

An hour later I was recalled to the room, where, to my dismay, the Rector sat in conversation with Madame. The matter to my idea had now assumed a terrible importance, and I became thoroughly nervous.

"The Rector wishes to know all about this writing; be good enough to tell him from the beginning," said Madame.

So I repeated the story I had told her, and then was subjected to a series of cross-questions.

What books had I read bearing on this subject?

I did not remember reading any except the Bible, and the books we used in school.

"Have you ever written any such essays before you came to school?"

"No." I was sure of that.

"What makes you suppose then that you have written this?"

"It is my own hand-writing, and it is on the paper I took to bed with me."

"Did you ever do anything when you were asleep that you could not remember when you awoke?"

I hesitatingly answered "Yes." I knew that I had gone into my brother's room several times but had not believed it till he once awakened me there. And once I cut my hand, which a servant bound up, but I knew nothing of it till I awakened next morning; and people had told me that I used to walk in my sleep when I was younger, but I thought I had grown out of the habit now.

"But you have never done any of your lessons or your exercises in your sleep?"

"No."

"Then how do you account for your doing so on this occasion?"

"I don't know, only I had prayed so that God would help me to find thoughts that I think perhaps He helped me when I slept.

I don't know any other way it could have been done."

Some conversation ensued between Madame and the Rector, in which I heard allusions to a similar circumstance which had happened in some foreign land, where a young over-worked student had written a very learned treatise on some scientific subject, which was afterwards of the greatest possible value. In the end the papers were handed to me with instructions to copy the essay carefully, and send it in with the rest of my work.

"It is a very unusual circumstance," said the Rector as he gave me the papers, "but as it is undoubtedly your own hand-writing and as Madame Whittingham tells me that she has never had any reason to doubt your perfect truthfulness and honesty, we have no right to reject this, strange as it is. We have heard of similar occurences, and though various theories have been put forward to account for them, I am inclined to accept your own explanation of it and say that God helped you because you prayed Him to do so."

Never did a heart beat more joyfully than did mine, as, clasping the precious papers to my breast, I ran to the little study to begin the work of copying them. I seemed to have won a victory. I had been acknowledged truthful and honest. The Rector's voice had been very mild, and both he and Madame had looked very kindly at me when I thanked them with tearful but happy eyes when they gave me the papers.

On the day of the examination the usual programme was gone through; the songs, solos, piano-playing, and exhibition of drawings underwent the usual inspection. Then came the reading of the essays. All were accorded their meed of praise, for all were more or less good.

After this the Rector came forward and explained that the essay about to be read was, he considered, a direct answer to prayer. It had not been placed among the competing ones, as that would not have been fair to the others, but it was in his opinion worthy to be considered a very beautiful production, and he would therefore take the liberty of reading it.

This he did. But I don't think it created much comment except from those on the platform. All were tired of the morning's work and the close warm school-room. All the pupils were more or less excited at the prospect of going home, many of them for good.

I received many kind words from the Rector and the teachers, and a writing-desk well furnished as a special reward, though I do not quite know what for, for I had been told that, although undoubtedly the best, my essay could not take part in the competition by reason of the circumstances attending its production.

That, however, did not affect me in the least. I was perfectly happy and more than content with the commendation bestowed upon me.

CHAPTER VI.

THE FORTUNE-TELLER.

"Too curious man! why dost thou seek to know
Events which—good or ill—foreknown are woe?

. . . . . .

Even joys foreseen give pleasing hope no room,
And griefs assured are felt before they come—."

DRYDEN

IT WAS during the latter part of my schooldays that an incident occurred which, though not exactly belonging to the category of experiences I intended to relate, seems to me to bear some likeness or relationship to them. I was spending a few days of one of the holidays with a schoolmate, a girl only a year older than myself in years, but considerably older in worldly experience. She had been visiting some cousins and from them she learned that somewhere in the neighbourhood of—I think—Bloomsbury, there dwelt a mysterious lady who had the power of looking into and telling the future. "Not a regular fortune-teller," said Alice "but much cleverer and quite a lady—lives in a fine house, has servants and all that. My cousins said she had told them the most wonderful things."

"I thought it was only gipsies who told fortunes," I said, deeply interested.

"Oh, this is something very different. My cousins told me quite fine people went to consult her about their business or their troubles. I have got the address, would you like to go?"

What school-girl could resist such a temptation? Certainly not I. Before we slept that night we had discussed ways and means, enquired into the state of our finances, and laid plans for paying a visit to the mysterious lady. Alice did not know what it would cost to lift the veil of the future and we had considerable misgivings as to whether or not our united resources would suffice. But we decided to put it to the test. And the next day saw us *en route* for that part of London where the lady resided.

At this distance of time I cannot remember her name nor the name of the street. In fact I am not sure I ever knew them. It was Alice who acted as cicerone and guide, in virtue of her supposed acquaintance with the Metropolis, and the dignity which her seventeen years gave over my sixteen.

Arrived at the house, we were ushered by a boy in buttons and Eton jacket into a room which seemed to us dark as a tomb after the bright sunlit streets, and I felt a little cold shiver and thrill of awe, as I gazed round. The room was an octagon, hung around with dark curtains which shut out most of the light from the windows. In the many corners between the curtains were long narrow mirrors reaching from floor to ceiling. When we entered, it seemed to me that the room was filled with people, and it was only when our eyes grew accustomed to the semidarkness that we discovered they were our own reflections. There was something strange in the aspect of the room, and I began to wish I had not come, but kept this feeling to myself, for the boy returned saying the lady would receive one of us.

"You go Alice," I said; so she went leaving me alone in the gloomy apartment for what seemed to me to be ages.

When at length she returned, I had grown accustomed to the half light, and could see how pale and disturbed she looked. I felt more nervous and frightened than ever.

"What is the matter? Oh Alice, what is she like? What did she tell you?"

"Nothing much; I believe it is all rubbish, but it is your turn. The boy is waiting. I will tell you afterwards."

It was with a curious mixture of fear and a desire to laugh, that I followed the page up a flight of stairs and into a room over that in which I had been waiting. As far as I could discern in the gloom the room was similar in shape and furnishing to the one below, but I could not describe anything in it save the woman with long light or white hair hanging loosely over her shoulders in thick wavy masses. She was dressed in black, her face was pale and suffering, but whether she was young or old I could not, if my life had depended on it, have decided. I seemed to have an impression of something black and white and altogether mysterious, and felt an almost irresistible desire to rush out into the sunshine again. Whether it was due to my excited imagination or not, I had a sense of something weird and uncanny in the sight of that black-robed, white-haired woman.

My pulse beat like hammers. I wanted to laugh or cry, I scarcely knew which.

She glanced at me for a moment, then told me to be seated. I looked round for a chair, and seated myself on the edge of the nearest one I saw.

"What is that mark on your arm?" she asked abruptly. I looked hastily at the sleeves of my jacket, but seeing nothing, I stammered out something to that effect. She did not heed, but continued talking rapidly; I could only catch a word now and again, and wondered what she was talking about. It was some few minutes before I realized that it was my "fortune" she was telling.

In vain I tried to follow her and gather the meaning of her words: the more I tried the more bewildered I felt. She spoke rapidly in a droning monotonous voice, like that of a person reading aloud to herself. Once I caught a sentence or two having reference to a mark on my arm and its signification; then she stopped, and, looking at me fixedly for a second or two, said abruptly:—"You have eyes that see things to which others are blind. God help you! Your life will not be an easy one."

Then she resumed the previous monotonous tone, but I could not follow her; her remark as to my eyes had caused my thoughts to wander, and it was not till she stopped speaking, that I realized that my "fortune" was told.

After a pause she enquired if I had any questions to ask.

Yes, I had a hundred questions, but not one could I call to my mind at the moment.

"Yes, I want to know"—and I hesitated, wondering what I wanted to know most.

"If you will be married, perhaps?" she suggested.

"Yes."

"You will be married in two years or less."

Again I tried to stammer forth a question.

"You have not yet seen the man you will marry."

Another pause during which I tried to gather my wits about me, for the precious minutes were slipping away and there was so much I wanted to know. Before I could speak however she continued:—

"Your life will be a strange and eventful one, more so than ordinary lives. Much will happen to you, much misery, much suffering; troubles such as few know will befall you. But you will have more happiness than falls to the lot of most women. Your path is one of thousands,—beset with dangers such as few experience, yet in your hands will lie the power to guide and lead others to happiness."

She said much more, words of advice and warning given in a kindly serious tone. I felt the tears in my eyes and a lump in my throat. Then she paused and briefly told me I could go.

I rose from my seat, timidly wondering if I ought to shake hands before I left the room, but she passed her hand over her eyes as if tired, and struck a hand-bell which was answered by the entrance of the page, who held the door open for me. So, dropping a curtsey in school-girl fashion, I went down stairs to rejoin Alice, who greeted me with the words,—"What a long time you have been! We must hurry back."

Alice was unusually dull and silent on the homeward journey, but at last she roused herself to talk with the greatest contempt of all fortune-tellers, whom she declared she did not believe in.

"What did she tell you?" I asked.

"Nothing but a heap of rubbish; I can't remember half of it."

"Neither can I; I didn't know at first what she was talking about, and then, when I did, I'd lost all the first part and couldn't understand the rest. But she told me afterwards that I should be married in two years to someone I'd not yet seen. Did she tell you anything like that?"

"No, she said I should not want to marry."

"Goodness! is that true? Don't you want ever to be married?"

"Of course, silly! I'm going to be married. Why, I'm engaged now."

This astounding statement changed the current of our conversation, and it was not till we arrived home that I suddenly remembered the woman's remarks as to a mark on my arm, and asked Alice if she had told her of this.

"I? No. I know nothing of it. What is it?"

Now, it is a curious fact that on my left arm below the shoulder is a small mark shaped like a cross, which, although generally invisible, is at times of a bright red color, perfectly distinct to both sight and touch. As it happened, it was quite apparent at this particular time, though how it could be discerned through the sleeves of my dress and jacket was a question I could not answer.

It was not till some time afterwards that Alice told me confidentially, that the fortune-teller had predicted an accident in which she would suffer severely; "or die, I suppose she meant" added Alice. Then I remembered the pallor I had noticed when she returned from her interview with the white-haired woman, and the disbelief she afterwards expressed in the latter's ability to read the future.

The woman's words, as far as I remembered them, made a deep impression on me at the time; and for long afterwards her remarks as to my eyes seeing more than others' eyes constantly recurred to me and gave me a good deal of comfort, as they seemed almost to imply that this peculiar ability was not altogether an unknown one, and it led me to cherish the hope that after all it might not be a symptom of mental derangement.

Alice and I left school at the same time and never saw each other again, for shortly afterwards, she met with a horrible death.

She was at Brighton for the bathing season, when one night a fire broke out and the hotel in which she was staying was burned to the ground. Poor Alice, together with one of the servants she had tried to help, was burned to death. The fortune teller's prophecy that she would not want a husband was therefore fulfilled in a terrible manner.

The prediction, as to my marriage came also to pass, for in two years from the date of the visit to the white-haired woman I was a wife. As to the rest of the prophecy respecting my future my readers may judge for themselves in what measure it has been fulfilled.

CHAPTER VII.

MY SHADOW PEOPLE AGAIN; AND TABLE-RAPPING.

> "Shadows tonight
> Have struck more terror to the soul of Richard
> Than can the substance of ten thousand soldiers,
> Arm'd in proof." SHAKSPEARE

IT WAS during the first days of my married life that my dream people began again to haunt me. Transplanted from the midst of my small noisy brothers and sister, from the busy life of elder sister, nurse, and governess to four obstreporous, mischievous young ones, to the solitude of my new home, alone for the greater part of the day with very little to occupy my time, I was horrified to find that the old fancies of seeing people about me returned in full force.

In vain I tried other means of employment, sewing, reading, writing. Many times, in the midst of my reading or sewing, I would feel absolutely certain that some one was looking over my shoulder, or watching me from the opposite side of the room, or sitting beside me looking me through and through. In vain I told myself it was weakness to encourage such fancies, they would not leave me, till at times in desperation I have flung down my work and huddled myself up on the sofa, covering my eyes with a rug to hide the shadowy forms from my sight.

Sometimes I would reason with myself, laugh at myself, and then go boldly through the rooms searching every nook and cranny for anything which could possibly give rise to these vague terrors, saying to myself—"Now you see there is nothing there to be afraid of, nothing that looks like a human creature, either real or unreal; so don't be stupid and ridiculous." But in spite of myself these shadow people forced themselves on me, till the thought of having to spend long days alone was terrifying to me.

I had no friends, and very few acquaintances, in the place, most of my friends being in the south of England, so that I had very few sources of amusement or companionship.

The constant repetition of these visions alarmed me greatly. On one occasion I mentioned something of my dislike to being left alone, and of the curious sensation of being watched by intangible presences, but the consolation I received reminded me very forcibly of the Doctor's remark in my childhood, and the old fear and anxiety assailed me anew. I was constantly watching my sensations, comparing the experiences of one day with another, one week with its predecessor, the present month with the last to know if the mental malady with which in my secret heart I believed myself to be afflicted was progressing, if the weakness was becoming greater—wondering meanwhile how long I could succeed in hiding my state of mind from others.

Sometimes for days together there would be no recurrence of these visions; then my spirits would rise and I would sing and dance for very lightness of heart, thinking the dark cloud which threatened me was passing over. But in the midst of my hope, I would be startled into a half swoon by a face or form gazing at me from behind a curtain, or vanishing through one doorway as I entered a room by another.

It was during this time that I first heard the subject of spiritualism mentioned. It came about in this way. I was paying a visit to a friend who resided at some little distance from my home, when, in the course of conversation, she confided to me her anxiety on account of her husband's growing interest in, and visits to, a circle of spiritualists and their mediums. He had, she said, left her alone on several occasions for the whole evening until late into the night, at which she felt very much aggrieved. Listening to the descriptions with which she regaled me of the doings at these meetings, of dark rooms, moving tables, flying musical boxes, trance speaking mediums, I certainly considered she had a right to complain, and I wondered very much that a man with ordinary common sense should be for a moment entertained by such vulgar exhibitions of the juggler's art.

Taking the first opportunity of reasoning with him, I was astonished to find that he was inclined to view these absurdities with some seriousness and that my expostulations only provoked dissertations on spiritualistic hypotheses and descriptions of the manifestations. Sorry and annoyed at the easy credulity which he seemed to exhibit, I brought forward every argument I could think of to show how utterly preposterous the spiritualistic ideas were, how easily all the manifestations he spoke of could be performed in the darkness which was said to be a necessary condition for their production, and how ridiculous it was, of any one with a grain of common sense, to believe that a table could of itself walk about and intelligently answer questions put to it. The only answer to my tirade was an invitation to try and see for myself, which I promptly declined.

I did not believe there was any truth in the statement that pieces of furniture could move of themselves. And if it were true, then it was wicked. With this logical conclusion, I refused to discuss the matter further. During the following days my thoughts frequently reverted to my friend's strange credulity, which had pained and disappointed me not a little. From the time we first met at Sunday school I had always had a sincere respect for his genuine uprightness, his honorable and truth-loving character and his calm cool judgement and reasoning powers, which made his opinion in general matters sought for and valued. That he should for one moment give a serious thought to such a subject affected me very unpleasantly, and I tried to think over what arguments I could bring to bear on the matter when I should see him again. The more I thought of it, the more horrible seemed the delusion, and the more necessary it was that he should be convinced that it was all utter nonsense.

At the next invitation to "try and see for myself," I put aside the aversion which I felt to humouring him, even though it might be for a good purpose, and consented in company with two or three visitors to the house, to place my hands on a little table. They evidently thought it good fun, and were full of laughing expectation, but I could not find any amusement in it. I was calmly confident that my friends would see the absurdity of the assertion that the table would exhibit any signs of intelligence.

To my surprise, and perhaps disgust, there seemed to be a trembling vibrating movement in the wood of the table-top, which gradually spread itself to all parts of it, till it became more and more pronounced and at last culminated in a regular rocking movement. Seeing this, Mr. F. began asking questions, telling the table to rap once with one foot in answer for "no," twice for "uncertain", three times for "yes." Various questions were put and answered more or less truthfully; then said Mr. F. to me:— "What do you think of it now?"

"I think you are moving it," I replied, and just as I spoke, my chair with me sitting on it slid across the room and wriggled itself up on the sofa. I jumped down and half angrily, half laughingly, charged Mr F. with using wires or magnets, at the same time requesting him to withdraw from the table. Thereupon he not only left the table but went out of the room, and I locked the door to prevent him returning. I then seated myself in company with my other friends a second time at the table. Again my chair slid over the floor, and when it could go no further because of the sofa it lifted itself and me on to it as before.

At my request one after the other of my friends moved away till I alone was left with my fingers on the table top. Still it moved. When no questions were asked it rocked about, lifting first one foot then another, twisting half round as it did so, and in this manner made the circuit of the parlour, I following with my finger tips pressed on its surface.

There appeared to me to be something "uncanny" about it. Sometimes it shook with what one might imagine to be suppressed laughter, sometimes it gave one the impression of its being a living creature breathing with a gentle heaving motion. Then again it would make a sudden jump as if to wrench itself from under my hands.

As I went home that evening, very much perplexed at the result of the experiment, I remembered that Mr. F. had sometimes amused us with little exhibitions of mesmerism, and with that remembrance a possible solution of the mystery of the movements of the tables and chairs suggested itself to me. If it were possible to influence persons by magnetism and make them obey his will, was it not also possible that inanimate objects such as tables and chairs could be brought under the same power, and made to move or act in accordance with the will of the operator? I had never heard of such a possibility but that was no reason why there might not be some ground for the supposition. The more I reflected on it the more likely it seemed, and in discussing the idea with the others, who had assisted at the table turning experiment, it was decided to set the question at rest, by meeting the next evening and trying again without informing either Mr. or Mrs. F. of our intention.

Accordingly the following evening saw us assembled in my home, six persons in all, including myself. We decided that it would be better to use a plain unpainted kitchen table, as being more steady on its legs and less liable to be moved by any uncon-scious pressure of our hands than the small round three-legged one we had used the previous evening.

We seated ourselves around the uncovered table, two on each side, and one at each end. We placed our hands on its surface, joining our fingers to make a complete chain. It was not long, perhaps half an hour, before the same trembling and vibratory sensations were felt, at first apparently under our fingers, then communicating itself to the whole table, which began shortly to have a rocking, or more correctly a waving, motion without actually moving from the floor.

————————

CHAPTER VIII.

THE TABLE BETRAYS SECRETS.

"Is it thy spirit that thou send'st from thee
So far from home into my deeds to pry,
To find out shames and idle hours in me?"

SHAKSPEARE

WE began to ask questions, using the same signals as Mr. F. and received answers by the rocking movements. Some one objecting that these movements were indistinct and easily misunderstood, the table to our surprise lifted itself on one side gently from the floor and rapped with one foot clearly and unmistakably.

We put innumerable questions of a more or less absurd character. One gentleman I remember made particular enquiries whether the table knew of any hidden treasure which it could help him to find. We asked our ages, date of birth, the hour of sunrise and sunset, price of corn, in fact anything which came uppermost. The answers were I believe generally unsatisfactory though some were correct. At length we had exhausted our stock of enquiries and asked each other: "What question shall we put to the table next?"

Suddenly I said:—"Do you know where my father is this evening?" and the answer came promptly, by three distinct lifts of the table, "Yes."

Now, rather strange to say, none of us knew where my father was just at the time, and we were anxiously awaiting news of him. My mother was suffering from an internal complaint and had journeyed from London to the City of Durham to consult a specialist. He had given it as his opinion that an operation was necessary, and my father had been informed of this and asked to come to her to consult as to the advisability of having the operation performed, as my mother felt nervous about deciding without his presence. To this letter there came no answer. A second, even a third, was sent off with the same result. The only conclusion we could come to was that he had been called away, after my mother had left home and had not received the letters. In a note from her that morning she asked me to come to her the following day, as she was getting quite uneasy at not hearing from papa. Hence my question to the table and surprise at the answer.

"Where is he then?" was our next inquiry, but here a difficulty arose. Our signals only extended to "yes" or "no" and "dont know" and this was a question that could not be answered by any of these words. Some one volunteered to repeat the alphabet and the table agreed to lift a foot at the letters which formed the name of the place it wished to mention. After a good many mistakes, repetitions, and hinderances, we got the word "Swansea."

"Do you mean that he is in the town of Swansea in Wales?" we asked.

"Yes."

"How long has he been there?" (Ten knocks.)—"Does that mean ten days?"

"Yes."

"Impossible, that cannot be true. We know he was in London since that time."

(Ten knocks again.) "Are you quite sure it is ten days?"

"Yes."

"What is he doing there?"

"Dont know."

"Is he at some hotel?"

"No."

"Visiting at some friends?"

"No."

"That is too stupid. If he is not at any house or hotel, he cannot be there."

"Yes."

"Where then?" Here some one suggested "ship."

"Yes."

"Do you mean that he is on a ship?"

"Yes."

"What ship? What is its name?"

Here began again the repetition of the alphabet and after a while we got the name "Lizzie Morton."

"Do you mean that he is on board a vessel called 'Lizzie Morton,' and that he has been in Swansea ten days?"

"Yes."

"It is a strange thing," observed some one of the circle. "Have you any idea that he can be there?"

"No," I replied; "he was in London and was intending to finish some small business matter and follow mamma to Durham, but he has not come, nor has he answered her letters, but he is sure to have written if he had been called away anywhere. I believe it is all nonsense for a table to know."

"But" said one gentleman "they say it is a spirit which moves the table."

"Are you a spirit moving the table?"

"Yes."

"A man spirit?"

"No."

"A woman spirit."

"Yes."

"What is your name?"

"Mary E—."

That was my grandmother's name. "Are you my grandmother?"

"Yes."

"Have you seen my father in Swansea?"

"Yes."

"And he is there now?"

"Yes."

To say that we were surprised at the result of our table-turning experiment hardly expresses our feelings. For myself I felt quite bewildered, and not a little excited as well as puzzled, whether or not to tell my mother of what we had done. Next morning on the journey to Durham I was still wondering whether I should say anything to my mother on the subject and decided that I would not. The whole thing savoured too much of mystery, and I still had a clear recollection of the incredulous reception of my stories of my dream or shadow people, and shrunk from seeing the disbelief which, I felt, would be shown in her looks, even if she refrained from expressing it in words.

On reaching the house where my mother was staying I had scarcely spoken two sentences with her when she said. "I have had a letter from papa this morning; he is in Swansea and has only just received my letters about the operation."

I felt myself turn hot and cold, and the room seemed to go round with me.

"What is the matter?" asked my mother; Are you not well?"

I hardly knew what I replied, but in the end I related the whole story of our two table-rapping experiments. Whatever my mother thought, she refrained from expressing any incredulity and proposed at once writing and asking if the other statements were true, which was done.

I do not know if the letter was ever answered but two days later my father arrived and I met him at the station. On our way to the house he asked me who had been to see, or had been writing to, mamma as to his speculations.

"I do not know. I don't think any one has" I replied.

"Some one has" he said; "else how did she know about that vessel?"

"Have you really been doing anything with a vessel called the 'Lizzie Morton' then papa? And have you been in Swansea all this while?"

"Well yes; I have been there a few days about a little business connected with the 'Lizzie Morton,' but what is all the fuss about? I did not get my letters as I was moving about, until three or four days ago and have been very busy."

"Had you been there ten days when you wrote first to mamma from Swansea?"

"Ten days; oh no! I can't say exactly how many days, but not long."

"When did you leave London?"

"On the tenth."

"And you wrote mamma on the 20th: that is ten days."

"Well, yes, I suppose it is. Time goes so quickly when one is busily engaged."

Later on we understood the reason of his absence from home. Like most men who have spent the greater part of their lives on the sea, my father, in spite of his determination to settle down as a landsman, found the attraction to ships and shipping irresistible. He had on several occasions invested money in vessels and lost it, so that my mother had a wholesome fear of his being drawn into unlucky speculations.

Immediately after my mother's departure from London for Durham, whither my father had arranged to follow in a day or two, it chanced that he fell in with an old friend who was about proceeding to Swansea to inspect a vessel which was for sale, and he invited my father to accompany him. He nothing loath, agreed and they journeyed together. After having inspected the vessel a trial trip was made in it, and the preliminary arrangements for its transfer began. As he had said, "Time goes quickly when one is busily engaged'" and it was not till he had called for his letters at the post-office, where they had been some days awaiting him, that he learned how anxiously we were looking for news of him.

It was easy enough to get this explanation, but to understand how the kitchen table could know and, knowing, communicate these particulars was a problem not quite so easily solved.

"Depend upon it my dear" said my father, "there is witchcraft in it or devilry, one or the other, and it is better that you should not meddle with such things." At the same time he was quite anxious to try himself and get the table to move, and when, after repeated attempts, he at last succeeded he was much interested in the result. He afterwards told me very seriously that he believed the spiritualist people were more than half right after all, otherwise the thing was incomprehensible.

CHAPTER IX.

MATERIAL PASSES THROUGH MATERIAL.

It is the mystery of the unknown
That fascinates us; we are children still
Wayward and wistful; with one hand we cling
To the familiar things we call our own
And with the other resolute of will,
Grope in the dark for what the day will bring.

Longfellow

Puzzled and bewildered as I was, I could not so quickly throw aside my previous teachings as to agree with my father's conclusion. My friends Mr. and Mrs. F. were informed of the result of our experiment and its verification. After some discussion it was agreed that all of those friends who had assisted at the table-rapping described should meet one evening in the week for further experiments during the whole of the winter months, and see what would come of them. We were in all eight persons. With very few exceptions this arrangement was adhered to. We met regularly at the appointed hour on the same evening of each week, and in no case was our meeting barren of results. Sometimes distinct raps were heard on the table, and we obtained answers to our questions by their means. Sometimes messages were spelled out by means of the alphabet as at our first experiment; sometimes we put out the lamps and sat in total darkness, and frequently saw flashing lights, luminous clouds floating over our heads; sometimes a steady soft luminosity would be seen, but on trying to make out what these appearances were they faded away.

Sometimes we placed a small object such as a ring, a stud, or a coin, on the table and asked that it might be removed by this strange intelligence or power, we sitting and watching with our eight pairs of eyes. On one occasion a pair of links were placed on the table and we watched them carefully but they made no attempt to move. At length the raps or movement of the table—always the same plain deal kitchen table—took our attention and for a few moments the links were not noticed. All the time the chain of hands was unbroken and the alphabet was being sedulously repeated to obtain the messages from the table. At last we had pieced together the different letters and found they spelled the words:—"Look for the studs." Then we saw that they were no longer on the table. Our first thought was that, through the movements of the table, they had rolled off to the floor and a general search was about to be made, when we were arrested by further significant raps and after some time gathered that the links were no longer in the room but in an adjoining parlour. This we did not believe, as the door to the room in which we were sitting had been locked to prevent interruption when we had assembled, and had not since been opened. Then began a se-ries of questions to which, as in the well known game of forfeits, the answers consisted of "Yes" or "No." "Is it on a table?"

"No."

"Is it on the chimney piece?"

"No."

"Is it in a vase?"

"No."

"Is it in anything?"

"Yes."

At last we elicited that it was in a flower pot, in the flower stand at the farthest window from the door. Thither we all re-paired and carefully inspected the flowerpots, one of the gentle-men gingerly moving the leaves of the plants with the point of a lead pencil and the rest of us looking on expectantly. However no studs were there. This was the first real mistake the table had made and we wondered what we should now do.

We sat down again and placing our hands as before on the table solemnly informed it that it had misstated facts, and that the studs were not in the flowerpot mentioned, and that as they were valuable we desired to be informed without delay as to their actual whereabouts. After some little difficulty in getting into working order as it were, we were told that no mistake had been made but that the studs were really in the flowerpot.

"But we have looked in every one, and have seen for ourselves that they are not there."

"You have only looked on not in the flowerpots."

This was true enough, certainly no one had thought of looking in the flowerpots. Accordingly, having got to know which one we should examine, we all adjourned again to the next room and taking out the flowerpot in question examined it carefully. If I remember rightly the plant was a very fine geranium. There was no sign of any disturbance of the soil, which was quite hard and compact; but having, with some difficulty, turned over the mould, there, shining among the roots of the plant we found the missing studs. How they came there; how they had been carried through the closed and locked door; nay, how they had disappeared from under our eyes while we were seated at the table was more than we could hope to explain. In fact, I am not sure that any of us tried.

Returning with the links to the table we put them down upon it again and took our seats. Scarcely had we done so when they were gone again. This time we were told to look in a Japanese box on a high shelf. By mounting a chair the box was taken down and placed before us to be opened. It happened to be locked, so the key had to be searched for. On opening it the links were found inside a silver teapot which the box contained.

Again we were seated with the links before us on the table, but a third time they instantly disappeared, and after a long search, when we failed to find them, we broke up the séance to have a cup of coffee before separating. One of our friends, about to drink his coffee, had it splashed over his face. The links had mysteriously fallen, apparently from a height, into his cup, and we fished them out with a teaspoon.

To the most of us I think our experimental evenings were only looked upon as an amusement, or a pleasant break in the monotony of every-day life, and the spice of mystery in the whole thing gave our meetings a sort of piquant interest which other amusements failed to supply. At any rate, every time we met, something fresh was tried for, or something new was told us, so that instead of tiring, we were all desirous of continuing the meetings. For a long while it is doubtful if any of us looked at the matter with any seriousness, it was amusing, surprising and puzzling, but that was all. We were all young and took life lightly, and were well pleased to have some mutual interests, which brought six or eight good friends into frequent intercourse.

Mr F. was the reading one of our circle. He generally brought us some news of the spiritualist movement, which we received with mingled feelings. At first we were all more or less inclined to discredit the statements as to the wonderful phenomena attributed to the spirits of departed friends. To me, indeed, the idea was utterly repugnant. The movements of tables and chairs, the hiding of rings and studs, seemed too utterly trivial, savouring more of the tricks of fun-loving mischievous boys than spirits of the blessed dead, who, as all orthodox christians believed, were far beyond in the land which eye hath not seen, too happy on the blissful shores of the crystal sea, too busy in praising the Creator to descend to the dull old earth and provide amusement of so absurd a nature for us. It was not to be credited for a moment. Perhaps, however, these "spirits" might be the denizens of the nether world, the poor unhappy ones shut out of the paradise of the blest. But here, again, we could not reconcile the two ideas. The manifestations, if trivial, were innocent enough of harm; even the movements of the table were suggestive of a rollicking boyish fun that was impossible to resist.

No matter if we were depressed or otherwise out of temper, half an hour's sitting at the table would restore good humour and make us merry and talkative. Sometimes one of the circle would play a tune on a concertina, the others forming a chain round the table with their hands placed flat on the top. In a very few minutes the vibratory and undulating motion invariably began, gradually accomodating its movements to the tune which was being played. If it were a soft sad melody, the movements were also soft and rhythmical with undulations in perfect time. If it were a lively tune, the movements were quick, lively and decided.

A march or national hymn seemed to excite corresponding feelings, if one can so express it. "Yankee Doodle", in particular, always produced a wonderful effect, and was generally reserved by us for the grand finale, because the movements of the table became almost uncontrollable and generally we were all obliged to rise from our seats to accompany the table, which seemed eager to follow the player. There was no doubt whatever that the movements, vibrations, and undulations in the table while this tune was being played expressed pleasure and enthusiasm. On the contrary if "God save the Queen" were played the table just as unmistakably expressed a certain sullen dissent, either by remaining perfectly quiescent, or by heavy thuds on its surface, or by lifting itself and heavily dropping to the floor. A particular long-meter psalm tune seemed to be its pet aversion, and it was our great delight to get our musician to play it in as slow a fashion as possible. Then the table would writhe, twist, and turn itself almost upside down, varying the movements by short angry jumps, generally in the direction of the player, or by violent thumps on the floor that would have shattered a less substantial piece of furniture. In fact, it was not long before the once heavy well made kitchen table had to pay a visit to a workshop to get its joints fastened and undergo general repairs after our experiments.

All this was very amusing and we enjoyed it immensely, though my patriotism always disapproved of the reception which our national hymn received, and, in spite of the fun, I felt a little shocked at the anger displayed when the "Old hundred" was droned out. It seemed to me that, however atrocious the music, the subject was a religious one and I objected in my heart to its being treated lightly; though at the same time no one enjoyed the fun more than I did.

Sometimes we sang, in which case we were always accompanied by rhythmic movements or raps on the table.

Several methods were tried to facilitate the rapping out of messages. The alphabet was written on the table, and a pointer on a kind of swivel arranged to indicate the letters, but this did not satisfy us; the movements were uncertain and the messages unsatisfactory. In fact, what messages we did get were always received with a certain amount of discredit in consequence of a hoax or two of which we considered we had been made victims.

On one occasion a long message in French had been rapped out and duly noted. It was to the effect that a Madame Poltan or Poetan, living in the neighbourhood of Havre, was to be written to and informed that her son Jean had been drowned, giving date and name of place when and where the calamity took place. One of our circle undertook to write to the lady at the given address and in a carefully worded letter deliver the message. This was done, but we never heard anything more of the matter. The letter was never returned, but this we concluded was no ground for supposing that it ever found the lady in question, or, in case it had been delivered to a person of that name and address, there was no sign to prove the genuineness of the fact stated. At any rate we never heard anything more of the matter and no notice was ever taken of the message, which we had conscientiously delivered.

More than one doubtful communication had thus been rapped out, which had either been proved to be false, or which we had been unable to get confirmed, so that at last we gave up the attempt, and simply heard what was told us and formed our own opinions as to its value and kept it to ourselves.

True, against all the false or doubtful communications we received, there was one striking contrast, that concerning my father and his whereabouts, which as will have been seen was proved true in every particular. As it was, this grain of truth caused us to begin the experiments with the hope of finding more, and induced us to continue in spite of the discouragement we felt at some of the misleading messages we received. All the same, I began to find it dreadfully puzzling and to wonder what would come of it all.

———————

CHAPTER X.

FIRST EXPERIMENTS IN CLAIRVOYANCE.

"Very much did Zuma wonder
At the wisdom of his daughter,
When she talked of seeing visions—
Talked of wondrous things she saw—
Told them some strange thing would happen,
Told them such a man would die.
Then they said to one another:—
T'is not the voice of Y Ay Ali
It is not the child that speaks;
T'is some old and reverend spirit
From the land of the departed."

THE STORY OF Y AY ALI

ONE evening Mr. F., who had been telling us of some clairvoyant experiments he had read of, proposed that we should try in that direction instead of table-rapping. We agreed to his proposal and, the lamp having been extinguished, we sat solemnly round the table in the fire-light. But nobody saw anything except the fire-light dancing on the walls.

Mr. F. proposed at last that someone should place his hands over the eyes of each person in turn for a minute or two, and see if that helped; if not, then another person was to try till the round had been made. This was done by some of the members but no one saw the better for this blind-folding until Mr. F. attempted and, standing behind the sitters at the table, placed his fingers over the closed eyes of each in turn. Most of them thereupon declared that they felt some peculiar sensation in their eyes or head, and some said they distinctly saw light clouds before them, but this is not unusual if any pressure is placed on the eyeballs, so that our experiment seemed likely to be bare of result. I was the last of the circle to be blind-folded and, to my astonishment, scarcely had the fingers touched my eyelids before the fire-lighted room vanished, and I seemed to be in the open air, in a strange place, for I could hear the rustling of trees, the soughing of wind through branches; but it was black and dark and, though conscious of being somewhere on a country lane or road, I could see nothing. At the same time I knew that I was in reality seated on a chair, among personal friends in my own sitting-room. Yet even this actual knowledge did not in any way detract from the feeling of reality with which the strange experience impressed me. I knew I was seated in a fire-lit room, and that feeling or consciousness of safety never left me; at the same time I was equally conscious that the scene I witnessed on that dark country road was a reality and interested me intensely, in much the same way as one seated in a theatre, conscious of the fact of one's surroundings and one's own individuality, watches with interest and sympathy the scene being enacted on the stage before him. One knows that an actual scene is before one and that it is no dream or illusion. Very much the same as a scene in a play, did the scene opening up before me affect my senses, except that I knew it was not merely acting.

As I stood alone in darkness, feeling chilled by the damp heavy atmosphere and conscious of the peculiar scent of wet soddened earth and grass, a light suddenly flashed before me. I saw that it came from the open door of a house which I had not seen. The bright light seemed to proceed from an inner fire-and-lamp-lighted room, and spread itself out to the road where I stood. I could see the house, the road, the trees, lighted up for a moment or two. Then from the open doorway two figures emerged,—men. The door closed behind them and the darkness became as impenetrable as before. Yet in that brief space of time I had to some extent taken note of my surroundings, and knew in which direction the road led, on which side the house stood, that a ditch ran on one side of the road, and that at the far side of the ditch were trees. Dark as it was, I could with some difficulty distinguish the figures of the two men who left the house, and I followed them, not knowing exactly why I did so. One of

the men seemed to be intoxicated; he walked unsteadily, gesticu-
lated, and talked noisily or appeared to do so, for I could not hear
words. The other, a taller and more slender man, walked steadily
and helped his companion by taking his arm when he stumbled
in the darkness. All at once the shorter man disappeared; his
companion stopped, and halloed again and again. He got no
answer; he moved his feet cautiously as if feeling for the man on
the road; and called again, but obtained no answer. He seemed
uncertain how to proceed, and walked backwards and forwards,
searching as he went. Then suddenly he appeared to make up his
mind, and started off quickly. I followed. I saw a door open, and
he entered. Shortly afterwards several persons emerged from the
house carrying a lantern, the tall slender man with them. I followed them but nobody noticed me. They retraced the steps the
two men had taken, searching every inch of the way by aid of the
lighted lantern.

I noticed now what I had not seen before, that at a certain
point another road branched off from the one on which the
men were walking and ran along parallel with it on a lower level.
When the party had reached the place where the man had disappeared, a thorough search began; and I watched with great
anxiety for the result. At last one of the searchers approached the
embankment and, looking over, said something to his companions, whereupon they all turned back and retraced their steps till
they reached the junction of the two roads, when they struck off
on the lower one searching with the lantern on the side nearest
to the higher road.

At length they evidently discovered the missing man lying
by the roadside apparently insensible, and the searchers grouped
themselves about his postrate body. The taller slender man I
have before mentioned tried to lift up his comrade from the wet
ground, one of the others holding the lantern which lighted up
the group, and I now for the first time saw the faces of the men.
The features of the one lifting the head of the fallen man struck
me as being familiar, but for a moment I could not recall it to
mind. Then as they raised the man to his feet, he looked about

him im a bewildered manner. I glanced again at the man helping him and to my intense surprise I recognized Mr. F!

"Why it's you!" I exclaimed.

My astonishment at this discovery almost overshadowed my surprise at the strangeness of the whole vision. I had followed the various movements and incidents, in what seemed to be a little drama, with anxiety and with an apprehension that it might result in a tragedy. I had feared that the unconscious man found lying by the roadside was dead, and had felt greatly relieved when by the light of the lantern he was seen to be sleeping. All the actors in the scene so far as I knew were unknown to me, and although I followed every movement with interest and anxiety it was only as a stranger would have done, so that when I suddenly recognized Mr. F. as one of the principals it caused a feeling of almost consternation, so great was my surprise.

As I shook his fingers from my eyelids and facing him exclaimed:—"Why, it's you!" the surprise communicated itself to the rest of the circle, and question after question was eagerly asked as to the meaning of the whole thing. I had, during the enactment of the scene faithfully related every incident as it oc- curred, so that the others had followed it with almost as great an interest as I who, as it were, took an active part in it. It was, therefore, with no little curiosity that we awaited some explana- tion of the affair from Mr. F.

He told us that he recognized the whole of the circumstances as having occurred some twelve years previously, to himself and several friends who, having been during the day at a deer hunt, finished up at an inn before they separated. Mr. F. and a young man whose home lay in the same direction left the inn together. It was not until they had come out into the night air that Mr. F. on whom the wine seemed to have taken no effect, found that his friend was considerably the worse for the parting glasses and it was with difficulty he could dissuade him from returning to bid another goodnight to their comrades. He, however, succeeded in getting him some distance towards home when he suddenly missed him as I had seen. The rest of the story tallied in every respect with my vision. In some cases the minor details which had escaped his memory were perhaps only recalled by my relation.

It was with feelings very similar to those I had had with respect to our first table turning experiment, that I reviewed the peculiar vision I had that evening. To all of the circle it had a great interest, and the discussion which followed was eager and animated, but to me it meant something more. A great hope was born within me, which I hardly dared to cherish, that after all it might be possible that my shadow people were realities and not the result of incipient madness.

The hope, once raised, would not be silenced and soon became, though secretly, a great motive power which urged me on in the voyage of discovery on which I now fairly embarked, accompanied at first by all of the circle, till changes caused some to abandon the search, well content with what they had learned. Others left England, and one passed behind the veil which devides the spirit world from this, whence he frequently came with loving greetings and encouragement to his sometime fellow voyagers, who were groping slowly along in the darkness.

I began to read every printed page I could get hold of relating to spiritualism and spiritualistic phenomena, dreadful nonsense a good deal of it, which shocked and disgusted me. The communications purporting to come from the heavenly spheres were in some cases so devoid of even common sense, that had not some kind friends taken pity on me and recommended the works of Andrew Jackson Davis, Robert Dale Owen, and others, together with some of the best weekly publications, I should have abandoned the enquiry. One of the angel communicants I remember gave the information that there were plenty of vegetables in heaven—"as for cabbages they grow so large, so very large, that I cannot tell you how large they are." I do not remember the author of the particular work, in which this appeared, I think his name was Pine, and I believe he called it the "Spirit telegraph." I have not seen it since; probably it was not well received and soon died a natural death.

The accounts which I read of phenomena, wonderful and incomprehensible as they were, did not interest me so much as stories of clairvoyance. It seemed to me that somehow I possessed a clue to the understanding of this power, so that whatever I read of it, in some way fitted in with my own secret experience. I did not understand the vision of the men on the dark country road, nor do I think after the first few days that I tried to explain it to myself, but I thought that there was much to learn which would probably lead up to the solution; so it was better to begin at the beginning. Where the beginning was, where to start from, which road to pursue—were terribly perplexing questions. I could only read whatever came into my hands. Theories, Philosophies, Phenomena, Arguments for and against spiritualism, Denunciations bitter and violent on both sides, but especially against spiritualistic teachings; persecutions of mediums, Exposures and Impositions—it, was all very bewildering.

It was at this stage that I ventured to speak to my friends Mr. and Mrs. F. of my "shadow people" and my experiences in connection with my "dreams," for which I had suffered so much and often; and of the vague haunting fear which hung like a dark shade over my girlhood. It was to their kind sympathy and co-operation that I owed the light which chased away the cloud, and gave me courage to throw off the incubus which, being thus vanquished, seemed to shrink away and disappear into nothingness. As this vague trouble dissolved itself in the mist of the past, my heart, as the French say, became "like a little singing bird" freed from imprisonment. My courage rose, and I determined from very thankfullness to go on with the investigation and experiments which had led to my freedom.

———————

WALTER.

CHAPTER XI.

OUR SPIRIT VISITORS.

"The Great Spirit, the Creator
Sends them hither on His errand
Sends them to us with His message."

LONGFELLOW

UP TO this time our sittings had been held regularly. We had been kept amused and interested, but it had never been a question of any one of us having a special power.

The name of "Medium" was not an enviable one, so that when at last it was declared that I was the medium through which the results were obtained, I was anything but pleased and distinctly incredulous. My chief knowledge of "Mediums" had been obtained through newspaper reports of various prosecutions in which they had not appeared to advantage. To me, therefore, the name "Medium" was synonymous with that of conjurers, or impostors of a specially low class, and I was not anxious to be classed with them. The question was not insisted upon and our séances continued in the usual manner, until one evening the difficulty of obtaining straightforward messages was the subject of conversation just previous to taking our seats in the usual manner at the table.

We had all tried the psychograph with more or less success, but this did not meet all requirements, the process was slow and the writing indistinct. It was suggested that if it were really a spirit who wrote, he could probably use the hand of one of us as well without as with the aid of the psychograph. So the trial was made and one after another we took a pencil in the right hand and invited the spirit to write, we watching curiously for the result. In several cases we could see how the muscles of the arm and hand twitched, and the convulsive jerks of the fingers that held the pencil. Beyond a few scrawls nothing was forthcoming. Others who tried did not feel any affection in their hands or arms and soon resigned the pencil.

When it came to my turn I first noticed a tingling, prickling, aching sensation in my arm, as one feels if one strikes one's elbow; then a numb swollen sort of feeling which extented to my finger tips. My hand became quite cold and without sensation, so that I could pinch or nip the flesh without feeling any pain. After a few minutes the hand began to move slowly and laboriously, imitating the motions of writing; it made repeated attempts to form letters and, after a while, succeeded in writing a few large ill-formed, ill-spelled words. Another attempt resulted in a decided improvement; the sensations in my hand and arm, though not painful, were decidedly unpleasant, so that in spite of my curiosity to see what would come of the writing, I was not sorry to have a stop put to it by the clock warning us that we had been seated the regulation time.

The subsequent meetings were devoted to further experiments of the same kind, and it was not long before my hand became quite an adept in the art of caligraphy, and would write, rapidly and well, whole pages of clearly formed characters, while we were conversing or receiving messages. We very soon noticed that the handwriting had quite different characteristics, and not only the writing itself but the matter written had a very distinctly marked individuality.

These unseen correspondents of ours soon became familiar to us. We learned to know them by name, and they told us something of their history. One, John Harrison, an English gentleman who had lived in Yorkshire, lonely, misanthropical, with somewhat gloomy religious ideas and rather pessimistic, was given to long prosy discourses, chiefly on religious subjects, to which we attended politely; but it must be confessed that we felt relieved when another of the invisible writers took charge of the hand and pencil. This was Walter Tracy, an American. His story was, he told us, as follows:—He was a student at Yale University or College, and when the civil war broke out he enlisted as a volunteer and took part in several engagements escaping without injury, except shooting off a couple of his own fingers in consequence of carelessly handling his rifle. His friends desired him to recommence his studies when the war was over, but he did not relish the idea and wished to overrule it. An end was, however, put to the controversy by an accident which removed him to another world. He was drowned by the overlisting of a lake steamer when he and several other passengers were thrown into the water. He could swim, he said, but there was no chance among the clinging drowning creatures who grasped at him and dragged him down. Many years later I met a young man, also from Yale College, and was gratified to learn that in very many respects the little incidents related by him as to his life and experience were identical with Walter's names of places, masters, houses, and the traditions, customs, and habits of the students. According to Walter's own account he was about twenty when he volunteered and twenty two when he was drowned.

Walter very soon made himself a favorite with our circle; he seemed to bring with him a veritable atmosphere of fun, good humour and liveliness. It was he, he said, who made the table accompany the music; and after making his acquaintance through writing, we could quite see that it was in keeping with his character. He seemed as curious and interested in our experiments as we were ourselves and many times suggested fresh plans for our enlightenment and information. Sometimes we would ask a question which he would be unable to answer. After appearing to consider a short while, he would write:—

"I'll go and ask a fellow I know; stay till I come back."

And come back he always did and invariably with the information we had asked, but given in so humorous a style that it seemed more of a joke than the serious matter we had considered it. His fun-loving boyish nature was a constant source of amusement for us, and he was always a welcome guest, hailing gladly as we did the first sight of his large round bold writing.

In reply to a request for details of some particular subject, Walter confessed his inability to enlighten us, but added that if we liked he would bring someone whom he called the "Governor" who would if we were "civil" probably tell us all we wanted to know. But, he added, "You'll not have to talk to him as you do to me. You must mind your P's and O's. He is very particular." Of course we promised to be on our best behavior and treat Walter's friend with every respect, feeling a little amused at the implied reproach that we had not treated Walter himself with the politeness due to him.

This new addition to the circle of our spiritual acquaintances proved to be a very different individual to Walter or John Harrison. He was grave, serious and philosophical, yet kind, thoughtful, and patient; a wise student, a faithful friend, an untiring helper. It is now over twenty years since the evening Walter brought him to us, yet during all this time his friendship has never failed. In sickness, in health, in trouble, in ease, through evil report or good report, he has been ready with kindly advice and sympathy. From the first he constituted himself a self elected guide, guardian, friend, adviser, and mentor, never intruding advice, yet always ready to give it when asked; advice not always easy to accept, sometimes extremely unpalatable, sometimes so contrary to my inclinations that I have refused to follow it, though I must confess that in all such cases I have never failed to repent bitterly my waywardness. When I have followed his counsel, trusted to his guidance, all has gone well, never has he made a mistake whether in diagnosing a sickness, describing scientific facts or theories, or in his many statements respecting possibilities which had not as yet dawned upon the world.

We did not all at once realize the greatness of this new Intelligence which came to our assistance, but we soon found that we had scarcely needed Walter's admonitory warning, for even without it we should not have presumed to treat Stafford in the "Hail-comrade-well-met" fashion in which we indulged in the case of Walter himself.

On asking Stafford of his earthly life, he told us briefly that he was the son of an American politician and a German lady, educated for the greater part in Germany, interested in all natural sciences, studious, ambitious of acquiring knowledge, fond of experiments, an eager enquirer into all matters concerning the adaptation of natural forces to the use of man. His scientific

HUMNUR STAFFORD.

Copied from a pencil drawing done in total darkness.

career was stopped by an accident which rendered him incapable of rising from his bed to which he was a prisoner for three years previous to his death. It was during these three years that the question of an after-life began to interest him. Hitherto he had not troubled himself about it; if the subject had been mentioned he had considered it one which could not be treated in the same manner as problems of a mathematical or scientific nature. So far as he knew no proof of another life was possible, and theories impossible of proof were to him uninteresting and useless.

In his long confinement during which he found he could not pursue his studies, his brain, active and analytical as ever, was drawn to the subject of religious beliefs by his mother's tender efforts to give him comfort in his despair and grief at being struck down in the midst of his life's work. For her sake he tried to take an interest in her religion, and was surprised to find how much there was still left to hope for. He looked forward to death with something of the same anxiety and interest as an experimenter looks forward to the issue or developement of a plan of which he has been the originator, and which is to decide the truth of some darling theory he has fostered but scarcely dared to acknowledge.

He wanted what he had aimed for in all his studies—proof—and for that he was willing, nay glad, to die. He paid the necessary price and gained his object. He died and found proof, inasmuch as he still lived, his intellect unclouded, his love of study and desire for knowledge increased, his capabilities for understanding clearer and brighter, his human sympathies hitherto repressed now expanded, and he found himself as anxious to teach as he had been to learn.

This in short, is the account which he gave of himself. "Make no enquiries concerning my earthly career," he wrote. "You will discover nothing, I have not given you my full name. Many of my relations still live and I do not wish to cause them annoyance. You may accept my statement as to myself. It is true, as is also my desire to be of use."

In compliance with his wish we never made any enquiry, although opportunities were not lacking. Many remarks, incidental to subjects under discussion, betrayed his personal acquaintance with savants of different nationalities.

Later on, our circle of unseen friends was increased by a little Spanish girl who wrote bad English, interspersed with Spanish words. Her spelling was strictly phonetic, her expressions unmistakably those of a self-willed impetuous child of seven or eight years. She told us she was burned in a church in St. Iago, together with her elder sister. Walter she said was her great friend and she loved him very dearly. I fancy her affections were rather capricious, for she speedily attached herself to one of our circle whom she called "Georgio," and assured him she liked him best. From that time she seemed to lavish all her attentions on her new friend. If Georgio, for some reason or other, did not attend, Ninia either did not come or if she came was disconsolate. She often betrayed little incidents respecting Georgio's private life, very much to our amusement and at times to his unmistakable chagrin. Discretion was an unknown quality to Ninia.

"You should not tell people such things, Ninia," said Georgio sharply one day, after she had entertained us with a description of an interview between Georgio and a young lady of whom Ninia exhibited a decided jealousy.

"Why not?" she rejoined; "it is true."

"May be, but it's not nice of little girls to tell tales and let everyone know things not intended for them."

"Yo mus not do tings yo's shamed to tel pepels; dats wat Stafford tels Ninia."

In spite of her indiscretion Ninia would not permit any of us to make a remark derogatory to Georgio's actions. She seemed to reserve to herself the right to pose as his mentor and looked upon a comment from us as an infringement of her rights.

Faithful little friend! Some years later Mrs. F. and I travelled over a thousand miles to sit by Georgio's side as he lay dying. I had been sorrowfully writing a letter at his dictation, and just read it over to him. "Thanks" he said "that will do. I will try to sign it presently—Why Ninia! Dear little Ninia! this is good of you," he exclaimed.

I glanced anxiously at him startled by this expression of joy. His face was lighted up with a flush of pleasure and welcome.

"Dear little Ninia! don't go away again" he said, looking with longing eyes. Then observing our anxious gaze he said—"Such a dear little thing!—I am tired. I will try to sleep awhile."

Closing his eyes he dozed off into what we feared would be the last long sleep, with a more calm contented smile and restful expression on his face than we had seen for days. When he awakened he looked anxiously around the room and then his gaze fell on the space where he had seen his little friend before, he smiled and made a little sign of content. Several times he mentioned her during the next few hours. "She will get tired of waiting" he said once. His mind never wandered; he knew the great change awaiting him; and Ninia's presence seemed to give him courage to face it. He spoke to us quietly and calmly during the last hour and almost his last words were. "Dear little Ninia! Dear little friend!"

Sometimes I think of those first experiences of ours, when, tyros as we were, we thought it was useless to encourage such communications as Ninia's. How little we knew, how little we thought, that the small childish unseen visitor would become mightier than all the consolations of church and priest to cheer and lighten the path of one of our number through the valley of the shadow of death!

Yet still another spirit friend came and was made welcome at our little circle. This was a sweet retiring pure minded maiden whose name we were told was Felicia Owen, an English girl of about twenty, who at the time of her death was being educated in a Catholic school in Wales. What she wrote was always in verse, sweet and pure, bringing with it a breath from heaven. Once she wrote—and the words came back to my memory with irresistible force as I watched the dying Georgio—

"And when I came to die, it seemed so strange.

"To find a well-loved voice, a kindly clasping hand.

"To meet me, as I stood and trembled on the shore of that dark sea.

"Which flowed betwixt eternity and me.

"Yet this was so."

Felicia did not come very often to us; perhaps among our circle there were too few congenial souls for the shy gentle poetess. Perhaps as I had become the acknowledged, though unwilling medium for all these communications, I preferred that the writings should be on subjects of which I was ignorant. Not that I possessed the slightest ability to write poetry, but it annoyed me to hear that people thought "I could if I tried." So on the whole it was more satisfactory to me when the communications were of such a nature as no one could suspect a young woman something under twenty of being thoroughly acquainted with.

Sometimes my hand would write quickly and steadily for two hours at a stretch, while I kept watch on the paper as it was gradually covered with the small close characters of Stafford, or the large bold writing of Walter, and supplying with my left hand fresh sheets as required. Sometimes I read the sentences as they flowed from the pencil, but generally, if I became interested and anxious as to what would follow, the writing would become disconnected, words would be left out or misspelt, and the meaning would become unintelligible. My arm and shoulder would at such times ache till I felt sick with the discomfort and almost faint with pain, but I was beginning to value these communications too much not to bear these trifles patiently, even gladly.

By the sensations in my hand and arm I was soon able to distinguish the different controls, no two seeming to use the pencil in quite the same manner. Stafford occasioned me less discomfort than any of the others, although he frequently wrote steadily for a much longer time.

Sometimes a stranger attempted to use my hand and this was instantly perceptible to me; sometimes the writing would go from right to left as though the controlling or influencing power operated from underneath the hand. In such cases we had to read the writing reflected by a mirror. As a rule, however, our most frequent visitors were the five whom I have already referred to, except at times when we relaxed our exclusiveness and permitted some interested person to join our circle for an evening. Invariably at such times there would be an addition to the "spirit circle." Walter usually acted the part of master of ceremonies and introduced the unseen guest. In this way many interesting tests were given, as it frequently happened that the earthly visitant would be a stranger to the majority of us, who knew nothing of him or his affairs.

These casual visitors always caused more or less of an interruption to our usual proceedings, but we could not determine whether this was the result of fresh spiritual influences, or whether it was owing to the natural curiosity, or perhaps the natural scepticism, of the visitors. Some people seemed to bring with them a fresh influx of power; others, again, by their presence seemed to paralyze the manifestations.

A lady, who had been unremitting in her appeals for admittance, was one evening allowed to join us. We had been having a series of very successful experiments and assembled with a good deal of hopeful expectation, for we had been promised some special phenomena. We took our usual places, the lady visitor being placed opposite to me. We sat a long time, but to our surprise and disappointment the table gave no signs of moving nor could we obtain a stroke of the pencil. In vain we sang or played. In vain we changed the order of our seats. In vain we begged for some sign of the presence of our invisible friends, but no sign was vouchsafed to us. Every one complained of a feeling of discomfort, prickling, tingling in various parts of their persons, and one or two felt an unpleasant sensation on the face and hands as though cobwebs were being drawn over them. At last after nearly a couple of hours we gave up in despair. When taking leave, and on our expressing regret at our non-success, the lady visitor remarked triumphantly:—

"Do you know why your spirits did not come? I'll tell you. It was because I have been praying to God without ceasing the whole evening to deliver us from the power of Satan and to prevent his manifestations while I was here. You have had no spirit manifestations, and you may be quite sure you never will have if you pray, as I have been doing, for protection against the Evil one. That these manifestations are from the Devil you may be quite sure or you would have had your usual success to-night in spite of my prayers."

I had no arguments ready in reply to this. The lady was the mother of daughters older than myself; a good earnest hard-working church-woman, whose opinions on religions matters carried great weight, and whose self-imposed duty it was to look after the morals of all her acquaintances. She regarded our experiments with great suspicion and had not hesitated, in her conversations with me on the subject, to express her conviction that we were victims of the wiles of the Evil one.

And now this first failure in our experiments and her explanation of its cause nonplussed me considerably, and I looked on the idea of our having encouraged his Satanic Majesty in our midst with something like consternation! However after discussing the pros and cons of the lady's opinion we passed upon it the verdict of "not proven" and decided to proceed in our investigations and await further developments.

I did not know then, as I know now, how strong a weapon the will can be, and how disastrous to the success of such a sé-ance an antagonistic element may prove. We had all that to learn. Later on we could afford to smile at the opinions of those who gave the devil credit for so much and God for so little, but then we were mere tyros, and easily made afraid, but thank God, we had courage to go on and learn more.

———

CHAPTER XII.

SCIENCE AND SPIRIT PORTRAITS.

For such the bounteous providence of Heaven,
In every breast implanting the desire
Of objects new and strange, to urge us on
With unremitted labor to pursue
Those sacred stores, that wait the ripening soul
In Truths exhaustless bosom.

AKENSIDE

ONE evening, for some reason or other, we were sitting without a lighted lamp. The day-light had not faded when we commenced the sitting, but though it grew dark no one suggested making a light. Happening to glance over to the part of the room where the shadows were deepest it seemed to me that there was a curious cloudy luminosity standing out distinct and clear from the darkness. I watched it for a minute or two without saying anything, wondering where it came from and how it was caused. I thought it must be a reflection from the street lamps outside, though I had never seen it like that before. While I watched, the luminous cloud seemed to concentrate itself, become substantial, and form itself into a figure of a child, illuminated as it were by day-light that did not shine on it but, somehow, from with in it, the darkness of the room seeming to act as a back-ground, throwing up by contrast every curve of the form and every feature into strong relief. I called the attention of the others to this strange apparition, and was not a little surprised when they declared their inability to see either the child or even the luminosity of which I spoke.

"How strange!" I said, "I see her so plainly that I could draw her portrait if I had paper and pencil."

"Here is paper and pencil," said my nearest neighbour, and taking them I began hastily to sketch the head, features, and shoulders of the little visitor who seemed to quite understand what I was doing.

"I believe it is Ninia," I remarked, and the little creature nodded her head vivaciously, so that I laughed and expressed my pleasure, as I finished my sketch, and was viewing it with some pride. "Dont you think it is a good likeness?" I asked Mr. F. who sat near me.

"It's hard to tell in the dark," he replied, "we must get a light in order to judge."

Then for the first time I remembered that we were sitting in black darkness, and I began to think I had been asleep and dreamed of the luminous child-form and my sketching its likeness. I held the paper nervously fearing that the lighted candles would reveal a blank sheet of paper. But no! There it was; I had not dreamed. Ninia's face smiled at us from the paper as she had smiled at me from her dark corner. I had caught her features quite cleverly and felt very proud of my performance.

"I can understand your seeing the child" remarked one, "but I cannot understand your sketching its portrait in the dark."

Neither could I understand it myself. All I knew was that it was not dark to me. I saw the child, I saw the paper and the pencil, but gave no thought to anything or any one else; in fact, in a short while I did not feel at all sure of anything. I required to look at the sketch to be certain the whole circumstance had not occurred in a dream.

This new development was a great delight to me and the séance evenings were looked forward to with new interest. We asked our spirit friends to "stand for their portraits," and took our places well provided with drawing-paper and pencils. As it was now summertime it became necessary to darken the windows, and we found that the darker the room the better the luminous forms were defined. At least I found it so; the others seemed to remain obstinately blind to the presence of our guests.

During the next few months our evenings were fully occupied by the taking of these portraits. Sometimes the forms faded

The above is copied from a photo of the pencil sketch and writing under same.

The above is a copy of one of the unclaimed portraits drawn in darkness. Actual time occupied in sketching, about thirty seconds.

from my sight before I had transferred their lineaments to paper; sometimes I would succeed in sketching two or more portraits during the evening. If any stranger was at the séance there came, in nearly all cases, some strange spirits too, and I was frequently successful in making a sketch of them. Generally these sketches were instantly recognized and claimed by their friends. Those few that were not recognized I kept myself, but they were not many. Stafford, Walter, John Harrison, and Ninia were among the first and are still among my valued treasures.

The news of this fresh development in the way of mediumship very soon became noised about, and I found myself, much to my dismay, overwhelmed with visitors and correspondence. It seemed to me that all wanted portraits of their dead friends and considered that I need only shut my eyes and begin at once to supply them. Letters came from various parts of the world imploring my assistance, begging me to send portraits of some lost darling. At first I tried to obtain something to satisfy these bereaved ones, but, with very few exceptions, without success.

One letter I received from Egypt, from a Hungarian, who wrote that he was a spiritualist and was accustomed to hold séances in his home, and that he frequently had communication with a beloved and lost son. "This son" he wrote "tells me that if I send you a small article which had belonged to him he will be able to come to you and make himself visible so that you can draw his portrait."

A silk kerchief was in the letter and on my next séance night I held it in my hand. I waited patiently for what might appear, but for a long while saw nothing; then a slim figure of a soldier faintly showed itself against the darkness. This was not what I waited for, but for want of something else to do I hastily sketched in the outlines; however, before I could do more the figure faded into darkness and the sketch remained unfinished.

For several weeks I kept the kerchief by me during our séances, but without success. Then someone asked, "How old was the son of the man who wrote you?"

I did not know. "Then is it not possible that the young soldier whom you began to sketch was he?"

I had not thought of that, in fact I had all the time thought of a child. So I wrote to the father asking him for more particulars, but I never received any reply. And the young soldier's unfinished portrait remains unclaimed in my album.

While occupied with this strange work, portraying the features of the denizens of another world, I became conscious of my own shortcomings in the art of drawing, and began to spend an hour or so daily in improving what little talent I had, working steadily for some months; but strange to say, though the work I did improved in quality, my power of seeing these luminious figures seemed to decrease, till the obtaining of a portrait became a rarity, and seemed in some way to strain my nerves, causing a violent headache for a day or two afterwards, so that I was reluctantly compelled to desist from my attempts.

Certainly the power returned occasionally and for weeks at a time I was able to execute these pictures. Then again I would be prostrate for days after a séance, so that eventually, though I came to the séance-room provided with materials, it was without much expectation of being able to use them.

The circle had by this time undergone some changes. Some members had left the town, some had left England, and others had taken their places at the table. A few of the old members still remained, and had never failed to take the seats they had occupied from the time when our investigation began. One new visitor who had come to us in the hope of obtaining a portrait, or at least being present while one was being drawn, was the cause of a fresh phase in our studies. This gentleman, Mr. Barkas, was in his way a celebrity and a public man. He was well read in the various sciences, a lover of art, an intelligent and careful observer, taking great and benevolent interest in the education and culture of the working man. He instituted an art-gallery, reading-room, and library in Newcastle, and was never weary in seeking such objects, to attract visitors, as would tend to their education. In additon to this he frequently gave lectures on subjects which were for the moment occupying public attention; lectures which, however dry the subject, became interesting from his manner of handling it. No matter how large the lecture hall, it was always filled to the last seat with an attentive intelligent audience when he occupied the platform.

Mr. Barkas *F.G.S.* was a spiritualist. He did not intrude his belief in the existence of the spirit world on anyone, but it was a well known fact in spite of his reticence; and as a public man he was at times held up to ridicule in an unenviable manner, which he accepted with a good humoured nonchalance.

He became a member of our little home-circle in the hope of seeing something new, but for several evenings we were unsuccessful. At last, quite unexpectedly I was enabled to see and sketch the portrait of a sweet old lady who claimed to be a relative of his. He, however, did not recognize her except by the dress, which might perhaps belong to his grandmother of whom he had but a faint recollection. On one of these evenings, while waiting for what might come, Mr Barkas mentioned that he was about to begin a course of twelve lectures in a large hall in the neighbourhood. During the conversation which ensued, it transpired that these lectures were to be popular illustrations of the sciences. The first was on electricity—its uses and application, or something similar. Mr B. proceeded to mention the points of the subject which he would endeavour to illustrate to his audience by practical experiment, and spoke of different theories which had been held to account for various phenomena. During the conversation, to which I had been an attentive though silent listener, I had been holding a pencil in my hand over a sheet of drawing paper, ready to begin to draw should any model present itself. I felt my hand turn cold and numb; then the pencil began to write, and we read the words:—"May I ask what particular theories you advocate and intend to illustrate?"

"That is for me, I presume," said Mr Barkas, looking at me with a smile. "Are you interested in such matters?"

"No—yes—I don't know—I don't think I know anything about it. It is Stafford who asks, not I," I replied.

"Well then," said Mr B., "if Mr Stafford is interested I have no objection to tell him." Then followed a long explanation respecting different theories and their merits or demerits, concluding with a dissertation on the particular views held by himself,

Mr B. and his reasons for holding them. During this explanation I had endeavoured to follow it attentively, as it appeared to be addressed to me, but I very soon lost the thread as it were, and became utterly bewildered with the repetition of technical terms, and had no more idea of the meaning of the words than if they had been couched in Hebrew.

As soon as he had concluded, my hand wrote in a clear decisive manner the words "You are wrong. So far as you have gone in for experiments they would appear to bear out your theory, but go a little further; try the experiments which I shall by your leave propose, and you will find that it is not tenable."

Mr B.—"You seem to be well up on this subject; perhaps you can instruct me instead of my informing you?"

S.—"I know very little, but I have read and experimented somewhat, and these things are always of interest. It is possible I may have noticed things which have escaped your observation, and *vice versâ*; if I can help you in any way it will give me pleasure."

Certainly this was turning the tables in a very unexpected fashion on our learned friend. I fancy we all felt a little scandalized at Stafford's cool superiority, for none of those present would have presumed to question Mr B's knowledge, or the correctness of any theory he chose to uphold. At the same time, though I did not understand what it was all about I felt a strong but secret partisanship for Stafford, and was anxious that he might come out of the argument with success. I fancy the same feeling predominated in the other members of the circle, for when at the end of nearly three hours' argument Mr B. said "Well, my friend, I will take your advice and choose another subject for my lecture, and in the meantime will make the experiments you suggest and and see the result," there was considerable satisfaction expressed in the countenances and words of the rest of the sitters.

After this discovery of Stafford's erudition on scientific subjects, our séances assumed quite a different character. Mr B., who had been somewhat startled at his knowledge being questioned, had made the conversation known to some of his friends who were, if not interested in the "spiritual manifestations", sufficiently curious to see the "young woman of limited education,"who could learnedly discourse on natural sciences and point out fallacies in the conclusions arrived at by savants. These gentlemen solicited permission to attend our weekly circle, and usually came armed with a long list of questions on scientific subjects, which were evidently intended to bother the "young woman" rather than to elicit information.

Stafford calmly interfered and wrote:—"If I can be of any service to you it will be a pleasure to me, but let us have some order in our work and take one subject at a time."

"Will you tell us with what subjects you are well acquainted?"

"I am not well acquainted with any subject, but like yourselves I have read a little of several. If you mention the subjects on which you wish to question me I will tell you if I can discuss them with you."

"Then we would propose the subject of "Light".

"Well, and then—?"

"Sound, Acoustics, Music, Harmonics."

"And then?"

"Well, if we discuss these we are afraid your patience will be exhausted; if not we can take up other subjects afterwards."

Then began what seemed to me a contest of wits which lasted throughout several months. As Stafford had suggested, only questions pertaining to one subject were allowed during the same evening. Sometimes the one subject took several evenings to discuss and during that time the gentleman, who had the subject in hand, was fully occupied in correspondence with others in different parts of the country, verifying the statements of Stafford or in gathering matter on which to base his questions.

As far as I was concerned I took no interest in these discussions beyond a lively desire that Stafford might show himself capable of competing with the several clever men who were, as it seemed to me, desirious of proving their own superior knowledge. I did not understand the technical terms that were constantly used and I wondered sometimes if the questioners understood them themselves. Generally I amused myself during these prolonged sittings with studying the countenances of the various sitters round the table and speculating as to the amount of wisdom they were inbibing from all this learned talk.

One gentleman used generally to close his eyes and look as though he were struggling with some weighty scientific problem. Once, in the midst of a lengthy reply which my hand was writing, an unmistakable snore was heard proceeding from the meditating scientist, which so provoked my risibility that I had great difficulty in sitting quietly enough to let the writing go on.

Sometimes a question would be asked to which Stafford would reply:—"I do not know, but I will enquire and tell you presently." Then there would be a cessation of writing for a few minutes more or less, when he would again set the pencil in motion and answer the question.

Frequently at such times "Walter" or "Ninia" would fill up the intervals of waiting with funny remarks, or comments on the dryness of the entertainment and wonder whether we liked it. Sometimes I would be enabled to sketch the face of one of our spirit visitors but this was very seldom. The séances usually left me very weary and exhausted. My health was not good; domestic troubles and worries tried me severely and except for the intense interest taken in these séances I should have been tempted to give them up for a while. However, I had not the courage to disappoint the many anticipations indulged in by my friends and kept on as long as my strength would permit.

The four subjects previously mentioned were under discussion a considerable time. In connection with sound, Stafford described very minutely an instrument for carrying sound-waves to unlimited distances; this instrument he said would shortly be known to the world. His statement was received politely, as we were accustomed to receive all communications from him, but as one of the sitters remarked when speaking of the instrument later—"Those who live longest will see most." It was not necessary for us to become many years older before the Telephone was given to the world as Stafford had described.

Another invention which he told us would appear was what he called a "Designograph" by which a person using a pen or pencil at one side of the globe could, by means of some electric arrangement, reproduce, on paper at the other, his own handwriting, so that designs and sketches could by the same means be faithfully transmitted the length and breadth of the earth. This was a quarter of a century ago, but this last invention was only given to the world within the present decade and even now is not generally known or applied.

"Dear Stafford" said Mr. Barkas one evening; "we have exhausted our fund of knowledge in questioning you. Can you suggest any other subject of interest which may with advantage be discussed?"

"It is for you to suggest," replied Stafford.

"I am at a loss for a subject which would be of general interest" said Mr. B. with a smile, which made me think of my sleepy neighbour. "But there is a friend of mine, a doctor of medicine, who frequently asks to make your acquaintance; perhaps he may be able to suggest some interesting subject."

"I shall be pleased to meet any friend of yours."

Accordingly the doctor came and suggested the entertaining subject of "Anatomy" which was discussed with seemingly great relish for one or two evenings, the doctor and Stafford appearing to me to be vieing with each other in the use of Latin terms and expressions. After bones, the nerves came under discussion, and here Stafford seemed, at once to take the lead. Once he broke off in the middle of a sentence saying:—"Wait a little; I must ask a friend of mine about this; he is better informed than I." For half an hour we were entertained by Walter who in humorous mimicry of "The governor" gave us a scientific dissertation on the properties of the air which he called "Oxyhydronitroammoniac." On being asked what he meant he replied—"When I discourse on scientific subjects I prefer to use scientific terms," evidently intending this as a hit at the doctor whose conversation was almost unintelligible to ordinary intellects in consequence of his lavish use of technical terms.

Stafford returned after the lapse of half an hour, evidently well supplied with the information he required, and the discussion of the function of certain nerves was resumed.

"Willis tells me"—he began, when the doctor who was watching the words as they were formed on the paper, interrupted—

"Willis? What Willis? Do you mean the great Doctor Willis, the authority on the nervous system and its functions?"

"Yes, I believe he is considered an authority; that was why I went to him; some particular nerves of the brain were called after him he says.

"Dear me!" remarked the doctor, and it seemed to me that his respect for Stafford increased from that moment.

On the subject of music, which had been put off from time to time because we were not acquainted with any one sufficiently well informed to discuss it, we at last were fortunate enough to interest Mr. William Rae a clever and celebrated organist. I had been for a short while a pupil in his choir and had a very great liking and respect for him.

As I have elsewhere mentioned I had never studied music and did not take any more than a very superficial interest in it, so that the discussion did not promise any entertainment for me.

Stafford explained that he was not a practical musician, but had read something of the theory of music. Practical musician or not he soon exhibited a more profound and wider knowledge of the subject than Mr. Rae, who said that he would write to some friends to ask their opinions and suggestions and then return to the subject. Stafford consented and the following week Mr. Rae appeared with a long letter from Sir Jules Benedict, containing explanations which bore out Stafford's statements on the disputed questions.

The subject of music, harmony, and the various constructions of organs and musical instruments seemed a never ending one. In spite of my natural desire to be polite and accommodating to the good friends who were so much interested I grew terribly weary, and my health, never robust, threatened to give way under the conflicting cares which had for some time lain heavily on my shoulders. In all probability Stafford saw that I must have rest, and at the end of a year from the beginning of the "Scientific séances" he said they must be discontinued for a while and later on we could return to them. One subject had been proposed which had not been touched upon, for want of a questioner sufficiently at home on the subject, namely that of Chemistry.

Mr Barkas remarked that much as he agreed with Stafford that I required rest, it was a pity that this matter had not been broached earlier, inasmuch as one of the best known Chemists of the day, Mr T. Bell, had been making earnest enquiry for permission to discuss that subject with Stafford. But Stafford was inexorable; Mr. Bell must wait; the medium's health was of more importance than the discussion of any subject; consequently there was nothing further to be said.

Mr. Barkas closed his series of lectures by one on "Recent experiments in Psychology" in which, without betraying the identity of any one of the circle, he made public what he called the "Extraordinary replies to questions on scientific subjects by a young lady of very limited education."

I did not at the time feel particularly flattered at the imputation on my education, but, on taking myself to task for the feeling of annoyance, I had to confess that so far as a knowledge of the subjects under consideration was concerned, my education was distinctly limited, and I had no right to resent the remark.

The whole of the manuscripts as to these séances, although belonging to me, were retained by Mr. B. in order to publish extracts from them. After his death I obtained them, but at the same time a request was made that I should not publish them or his name in connection with them. I have, therefore, only alluded to what he himself published of these séances or at least to that which became public property.

CHAPTER XIII.

A GLIMPSE OF TRUTH.

"The conflict of the present and the past,
The ideal and the actual in our life
As in a field of battle, held me fast
Where this world and the next-world were at strife."

LONGFELLOW

THESE experiments which were carried on with few intermissions for four years or more were at last brought to an end. Death had struck terrible and heavy blows. Those who were nearest and dearest to me, whom I had loved best, were gone. They had passed on to the Shadow Land in quick succession, and I was left alone. I was worn out and wearied with the anxieties and troubles that had crowded themselves together on my shoulders till they could bear no more, for a severe cold which I contracted late in the autumn seemed to undermine my constitution and affect my lungs. My doctors, also, suspected internal cancer, and strongly advised a residence in a warmer climate if my life were to be saved.

Thus hopeless, listless, and indifferent, I journeyed to the shores of the Mediterranean. I had ceased to take much interest in anything. Weak and exhausted by grief and sorrow, life seemed to hold but little to care for, nothing to hope for. The doctors had said that unless some radical changes set in I had not long to live, perhaps three months, in any case not more than six; and so they had sent me away to the south to die. I was willing enough to go. I had lived my life and lost all that made it worth living for, so it was well to be done with it early. I had now no ties, and but few friends; my relatives, had been alienated from me in consequence of the interest I had taken in spiritualism; so that it really seemed to me that death for once would do well to cut off one whose interests and usefulness in life were ended.

But youth has wonderful recuperative powers, and health soon restores the love of life and paints the future in brighter colors. Almost in spite of myself I rejoiced when renewed strength sent the blood coursing more swiftly through my veins, and my nerves thrilled in response to nature's awakening under the sunny southern heavens. I watched the change from winter to spring from my sick couch, and it seemed to me that for the first time in my life I realized how beautiful the world is. The charm of the sunshine, the skies, the air, the verdure, came home to me with a new meaning. I stretched out my arms to it all with a longing to understand and be at one with nature. I felt new life penetrating to my innermost heart; hope sprang up from the grave where I had buried it as I thought for ever; and with a sort of exultant joy I felt how good it was to be alive, and thanked God for the blessed gift. Yet nothing had changed in my surroundings; only a sunbeam had glinted through the clouds that had gathered about me; and through the rift it made I had seen that life was not worthless because trouble and sorrow had come.

From that time I made rapid strides on the road to health, and with increasing physical strength I was able to gradually look my life steadily in the face, and also to look backward over the events of the past without losing faith in the future. Then it was that I first began to understand what spiritualism meant. Strange as it may appear I had somehow, in spite of all our experiences, never been able to accept the spiritualists' theories as a conclusive and unquestionable explanation. There was not one of our circle but called him or herself a spiritualist, but I had never been able to bring myself to this. Perhaps in my inmost heart I was one, only the difference between my early teachings and this new doctrine was too great for reconciliation.

The opinions of some professed spiritualists appalled me. Once in conversation with a well known adherent to the cause, the life and work of Christ were mentioned. To my infinite dismay he questioned the very existence of the "Son of man." He was a myth, an idea, not an individual. The existence of a Deity was also questionable. He was a bogey to frighten the weak, or a bait to entice the selfish, who would endeavour to serve him for fear of the consequences, or for the sake of rewards to be gained. All this was very terrible to me. My whole nature rose up in revolt. I could not accept such ideas. I read my bible more diligently than ever before, trying to reconcile its teachings with those of the spirits. Sometimes I would come upon words of comfort and enlightenment which I would seize with eagerness as upon a key to these mysteries. Then again I would fall back into the slough of despond and see no way out. I seemed to be as it were divided against myself, the one part holding fast to the old teachings and defending them at every point; the other besieging, assailing, and tearing down defences, leaving me worn out and weak with the inward struggle.

There was no one to help me with advice. Those to whom I applied would either not discuss the question or denounced spiritualism as the work of the devil. Others, "Agnostics" as they called themselves, though I did not then know the meaning of the term, treated the matter with philosophic calmness, and bade me not worry myself, or advised me to believe in whatever made me happiest and let the rest alone. "Whatever is, is" they said and no amount of belief or non-belief on my part could change anything, either for me or any one else in the world. Thus I was thrown back on myself to fight it out alone. In the opinion that these manifestations were from the evil one I could not concur. The character of the communications from John Harrison or the sweet poetry of Felicia Owen was a direct denial to this. In fact so far as John Harrison's writings went, their very religiousness affected me much as did our old clergyman's sermons. The concluding words of both were always hailed with a sigh of relief. Certainly there was no more of Satan in John Harrison than in our good old clergyman.

It was during these weeks of convalescence, when the love of life had taken fresh root in my heart, that I began to understand and accept the teachings of these spirit friends. How it came about I do not quite know. Somehow the quiet days, spent under the green trees, with the blue skies and sunshine beamimg upon me through the branches, seemed to make things plainer. I was not assailed on all sides with conflicting opinions and controversies. I was alone with nature and together we fought, together went over the old ground inch by inch. It seemed to me then, that those things which had been irreconcilable when viewed through the colored spectacles of doctrinal teachings, became in the clear white light of heaven united and harmonious.

Seen in parts the teachings would appear to bear no relationship the one to the other. As a whole they are linked together and form one perfect and glorious truth; much the same as in the brilliant coloring of an autumn leaf. Though its vivid green contrasts sharply with the rich crimson, yet the two are united by innumerable delicate gradations and shades of color, till it becomes a perfect dream of beauty and harmony, not one faint tint too much or too little.

So, while considering the teachings of the church, and the teachings of the spirits separately, I could only see the contrasts. It was only when by some mysterious inner process I was, as it were, given a glimpse through a clearer medium than the dogmas of churches or the individual opinions of professors of "isms," that I was able to trace the truth and beauty that lay between and joined the one with the other into a perfect and beautiful whole.

True, there were many things inexplicable to me both then and now; but I felt that I had found the key to a new world; a world so new, so wonderful, filled with a light so pure and clear, that I only needed to take my difficulties into its penetrating rays in order to have them softened down, smoothed away, or explained.

CHAPTER XIV.

SAVANTS BECOME SPIRITUALISTS.

"Properly there is no other knowledge but that which is got by working: the rest is yet all a hypothesis of knowledge; a thing to be argued of in schools; a thing floating in the clouds, in endless logic-vortices, till we try and fix it."

CARLYLE

WHEN one has made, or fancied one has made, a great discovery I suppose one's first impulse is to spread the news abroad, never doubting that the knowledge will be as eagerly welcomed and highly valued by the rest of the world as by one's self.

Much of the spiritualistic phenomena, as will be seen, had been familiar to me for some three or more years whilst some I had been accustomed to from my childhood, but belief in these manifestations does not necessarily make one a spiritualist, though it is the fashion to designate all such believers by that title.

Up to this time I had rather disliked being called a spiritualist, the name seemed to me without any special signification and uncalled for. That one believed in certain facts which were perfectly plain and clear to the most limited understanding gave no one the right to the title, any more than a belief in the existence of the stars and planets gives one the right to call himself an astronomer. On the other hand many of the truest and best spiritualists I have known have never in their lives witnessed any of the manifestations, which to others are the first necessary steps on the road to a better understanding of the laws, which connect the world of matter with the world of spirit.

I have known persons with a great experience of mediumstic or spiritualistic phenomena who had an unshaken faith in the genuineness of their spirit origin, yet who were, if I may use the words, materialistic believers not in spiritualism of which they knew nothing, but in spiritualistic phenomena. With respect to these persons I remember an interview with two ladies who called upon me. They were feeling themselves lost in a foreign country, and hearing that I was an Englishwoman and a spiritualist they paid me a visit. After dinner the subject of spiritualism became the topic of conversation. The ladies explained to my other guests, who by the way knew little or nothing of the subject, that they had been spiritualists for three or four years, had had séances with the best mediums regardless of expense, and had left no stone unturned in their investigation; they were as they themselves said: "perfect witches" for discovering mediums and never failed to interview every one they encountered.

At this juncture I felt infinitely thankful that they knew nothing about me as a medium.

"But" said one gentleman, "though all this is very interesting and very strange, I cannot quite see the need of it. In what way does it add to the happiness of any one to know that their dear friends have no better occupation in the next world than to cause tables to jump about, talk bad English through a medium, or to appear as caricatures, of themselves, as materialised spirits? The spiritualism of Christ seems to me much more beautiful and to those who believe in him it is sufficient for every need."

"Oh, yes, I daresay; but then you see we have thrown all that to one side; we don't believe in Christ; we want something more real and tangible than those old legends. Of course Christ was very good and, in the old times, very likely his teachings were sufficient but in this enlightened age we require something more."

The materialism of these Spiritualists was to me extremely distressing. Spiritualism to them meant phenomena and nothing more. Their professed belief was a very useful excuse for the non-observance of religious duties which had become a bore to them, and was also useful as a means for obtaining admission to séances to which only Spiritualists were admitted; but beyond these the name bore no meaning for them. Between these enlightened adherents to the spiritualistic cause and myself there was little or no sympathy. We went our separate ways seldom meeting again.

Probably they are still medium-hunting, though in the country in which they live their prey will not be easily caught.

That such differences of opinion could exist among adherents to the same cause I had no idea and the discovery perplexed me not a little. I was desirous of proclaiming aloud to the world the great truth I had discovered. It never occurred to me that the world would not receive the news as gladly as I had done. I thought I had only to tell people of my discovery to render them as happy as I felt myself, but somehow my statements were received with discredit. People listened politely, but declined to believe without actual demonstration. This I tried to give them, and it was then that I made a new discovery which seemed likely to upset all my plans for regenerating the world. The manifestations which during the years of experiments seemed to crowd upon each other, each one more wonderful than the last, needing no effort on my part to produce them, seemed almost impossible to obtain in the spontaneous ready manner in which they had always occurred. The power to write on scientific subjects, which had for so many months occupied our time and attention, appeared to fail utterly, and questions would be answered in so stupid a fashion that I felt very much provoked at times. The clairvoyant faculty, which in our own circle seldom failed, became uncertain and feeble; and the movements of the table were without any meaning which could be understood.

The facility with which all these manifestations had been previously obtained had quite spoiled me for bearing these failures patiently, and it was with no little dismay I saw the small result of my first missionary work, and began to realize that I knew next to nothing of the laws which governed these things. In some way, either by accident or good fortune, the persons with whom I had experimented had been peculiarly fitted for the work. Now that I was deprived of the material and support of their co-operation, the result of the manifestations depended as it were on myself or the uncertain help of promiscuous experimenters with less knowledge of the subject than I had.

Still I knew we had succeeded and would be able to succeed again, if only similar conditions could be provided. It was uphill work however and very disappointing in many ways. I wanted to convert the world, but; the world did not want to be converted. Eventually the world got its own way, as I decided not to force my convictions upon it unasked.

At the same time the missionary spirit was upon me and gave me but little rest. I planned and schemed ways for carrying out my desire to spread a knowledge of the reality of the spirit world and the means to communicate with its inhabitants, but they proved futile, either because people did not care to know, or I found myself powerless to produce phenomena which they considered satisfactory. It had never been suggested to my mind that anyone might or would doubt my statement respecting various phenomena, and it was excessively annoying to see the doubts expressed in a significant raising of the eyebrows or a shrug of the shoulders, even where my hearers were polite enough to restrain verbal comment.

I laid my difficulties before my spirit friends and asked their advice. They told me to be patient, not to try to teach others till I had learned myself; not to attempt to reform the world or set the church right, but simply do the work nearest at hand, and do it well.

Although I tried to carry out this advice it was often difficult to decide how to act, when beset on all sides by persons professing the most intense interest in the subject of spiritualism. It seemed to me wrong to refuse help even if I doubted the sincerity of their professions; I could only try and see. On the whole it was very discouraging work, and had it not been for one or two bright exceptions in the weary round of disappointments, it is possible my courage would not have held out.

After my health had been to a great extent re-established by my residence in the south of France, I made one or two visits to friends, spent a few months with Mr. and Mrs. F. who were then residing in Sweden, and afterwards accompanied some acquaintances to Leipzig, where, through the kindly offices of Mr. James Burns of London, the celebrated Professor Zollner was introduced to me, and it was owing to his kindly interest and that of his mother that my stay in Germany brought about one of the encouraging exceptions I have mentioned.

On the eve of my intended return to England, an accident happened which almost compelled me to accompany my travelling companions to Breslau instead of returning via Hamburg to England. I did not like this alteration in my plans as it was likely to upset many of my arrangements, but I could not, for humanity's sake, desert my companions under the existing circumstances.

When the change of route was told to professor Zöllner, he remarked:—"I have a friend in Breslau, my oldest friend in fact; we were boys together, and until very recently we were seldom at variance on any subject, but he could never tolerate my views on spiritualism; consequently a cloud has arisen between us which has to a great extent destroyed the life-long friendship, and although it grieves me, I cannot renounce my faith in spiritualism, even for my dearest friend. I. can only hope that he may at some time look on my views more leniently. If you could make him a spiritualist now, you would do me the greatest service; there is nothing in the world I desire so much."

"Very well", I replied half jokingly, "I'll make him a spiritualist for you. What is his name?"

"Dr. Friese" he replied as my train moved off.

The journey was a long one and the night was cool. In consequence of my hasty change of plans, my luggage had been sent wrong, and I was left with insufficient wraps, so that on my arrival in Breslau I felt very unwell, and went at once to bed where I was obliged to remain some days. One morning without any warning a gentleman was ushered into my room. I only caught the title "Doctor" as the maid opened the door, but naturally concluded it was a medical man whom my travelling companions had called I in to see me, and I at once began to tell him of my aches and pains.

"But my dear young lady, you mistake, my name is Friese."

"Are you not a doctor?"

"Yes, I bear that title, but not a doctor of medicine. I came to see you in consequence of a letter from my old friend Prof.

Zöllner of Leipzig asking me to call upon you.

This was a predicament indeed. I did not know what to say or do; my face was burning and I wanted to hide it under the bed clothes and relieve myself by crying. He saw my embarrassment and probably felt for me, because he began asking about the attendance at the hotel which he thought must be very poor, or such a mistake could not have happened. I told him how very little I knew about it, and that no one had troubled very much about me either one way or another. My friends had asked each day how I was and if I wanted anything, and that was all. As I did not feel to want anything but to be left alone they supplied that want perfectly.

I fancy Dr. F. must have used some very bad language. I didn't understand German, so cannot judge as to the words he employed, but the effect was marvellous. There was no lack of attention during the next hour or two. When the Dr. returned to my room he was accompanied by a medical man and the hostess of the hotel. The gentlemen discussed the advisability of removing me to the house of Dr. Friese, and the landlady protested against it saying there should be no want of care on her part in future. She had supposed that the other lady of our party had done all that was required or there would have been no neglect.

They seemed to me to be making a great ado about nothing, and I begged they would not give themselves any trouble on my behalf. The matter was settled thus. My travelling companions were wishful to proceed on their journey, and I decided to remain where I was till well enough to return to England.

They left next morning, and Dr. F. and his sister insisted on my coming to them till I had quite recovered. So I became an inmate of the Doctor's house. The winter was a long and tedious one and I did not get quickly rid of the cold I had contracted, so that my stay was indefinitely prolonged.

Dr. Friese was one of the most methodical men I ever met, and as soon as it was ultimately decided that I should not undertake the journey to England till the frost broke up, he drew up a plan for me to follow, as to my daily pursuits. I may mention that Dr. F. was an accomplished painter, and an enthusiastic musician. Above all he was a teacher. I do not think he could under any circumstances have refrained from exercising his schoolmaster propensities on any young person who came under his notice. He soon decided that the defects in my education must be remedied, and he set himself to do it, laid down his rules and regulations authoritatively and I most humbly obeyed them. And he not only made rules, but he saw to their being carried out, so there was no escape; in fact, nobody ever tried to evade them. He himself lived by the clock, and his household had to do the same. His rules respecting me were as follows.

7.30.   Rise—bathe—dress—with assistance of a maid.

8 o'clock.   Breakfast.

9 to 11.   Drawing or painting.

11 to 12.30.   Walking or skating. In the latter excercise he generally skated and pushed my sledge.

12.30 to 1.   Rest.

1 to 2.   Dinner.

2 to 4.   Drawing or painting.

4 to 5.   Walking if fine; if not, write letters.

5 to 6.30.   Tea, and short readings in German.

6.30 to 10.   Concert, or opera, if there were any; if not conversation on the subject of spiritualism.

10.30.   Sandwich and milk. 11. To bed,—no excuse allowed for sitting up.

In this way the days passed. I chafed against the monotony but to no purpose. At length one week of incessantly falling snow and rain put a stop to our customary promenades, and an interval in which there were no new operas played or concerts given released me from what was beginning to feel something like purgatory. The Dr. said he was determined to cultivate my musical taste. In vain I protested that he could not cultivate what did not exist. He would allow no excuse. To concerts or opera I must go. And I went willingly in the case of an opera, but with badly concealed unwillingness in the case of an instrumental concert.

During the days of enforced abstinence from music the time was spent in discussing spiritualism and in trying experiments, which succeeded admirably when we were alone or in company with one or two friends.

The Dr. was most interested in the automatic writing, and in spite of his love for musical evenings he acceded at last to my request to spend some evenings in writing and other experiments, instead of attending the concert hall.

CHAPTER XV.

CONVERTS AND CONVERTS.

"But human ignorance and prejudice shall at length pass away, and then science and religion shall be seen blending their parti-colored rays into one beautiful bow of light, linking heaven to earth and earth to heaven."*

PROF. HITCHCOCK

IT IS not necessary to relate the long arguments and discussions which were brought to bear on the subject of spiritualism, nor the many questions put to the spirits, which were answered chiefly by "Stafford". It mattered little whether they were couched in German or English, the replies written by my hand were equally concise, logical, and to the point. To me it seemed as though a struggle for the mastery was being waged between the Dr. and the spirit. One evening I remember the contest went on for hours till the clock, striking the hour of mid-night, reminded the Dr. that he had forgotten his usual punctuality, and had even omitted to eat his sandwich or to order me to my room. This unheard of circumstance seemed to occasion him a good deal of concern, for he remarked, *"This must never happen again."*

The next day or two I noticed that he was very thoughtful and distrait, allowing some very bad work of mine to pass without the sharp correction or comments, he invariably made over my crude drawings.

In the night I heard him pacing to and fro in his room, but when I asked if he were ill, he would reply: "I am well, but much perplexed." I began to feel perplexed too, and to wonder in what way I could help him, but he refused to ask more questions of the spirits or even to discuss the subject with me. This reticence made me fear that he was disgusted with it, and I was not a little afraid that not only was my half jesting promise to Prof. Zöllner likely to result in failure, but that the breach between the two friends would widen rather than be bridged over.

It was the third day of this strange silence, which was becoming almost intolerable to me, when the Dr. told me that I was to get on with certain studies alone as, he would be engaged for some hours at the university. He had to give a lecture he said.

It was nearly ten o'clock when he returned, and sent a servant to request my company in the drawing room for a few minutes. I went wondering at this unusual request.

"Do you know what I have done?" he asked when I entered the room.

"No."

"Can you not guess at all?"

"No," and I began to feel rather afraid of what was coming.

"Then I will tell you. I have to-night publicly declared that I am a spiritualist and tendered my resignation as professor in the University."

I was too much astonished to comment on this and somehow I felt sorry for him. I had certainly done my best to bring about the conviction of the truth of spiritualistic teachings, but it had never occurred to me that so much was involved. In spite of my pleasure I had almost a feeling of consternation at the sacrifice he had made.

"Was it necessary to resign?" I asked.

"Yes. In my capacity I was bound to uphold the teachings of the church and to punish any heresies or lapses from its doctrines. As a spiritualist I cannot do this, and therefore the only honest thing for me was to resign at once."

"Was it necessary to publicly acknowledge yourself a spiritualist?"

I felt a little ashamed of the question and more so when he replied severely, "Can you ask if it were necessary? What would you have done?"

I knew that I would have done the same, nay more! There was no sacrifice I would not have made, but all the same I could not help being sorry that he had had to make one so great and could only hope that spiritualism would make ample restitution.

The first work next morning was to write to Professor Zöll-ner sending him a newspaper containing the astonishing news of the Doctor's resignation and the comments of the press, which were, to say the least, not complimentary. The reply came in the shape of the Professor himself who had taken the first train which brought him to Breslau.

The meeting between the two friends was very affecting. They were neither of them young men, though the Professor was much the younger of the two, but in their delight in meeting and their reconciliation they seemed like two boys. They were so full of their new uniting interests that they reminded me forcibly of the time when the light had just come to me, and I had planned how to bring the good news to all my fellow creatures. As *I* had schemed and planned, so they went over the same ground. They would write books. They would give lectures. The name and reputation they bore would open the way to all classes, and people would eagerly accept the good news, because *they* brought it.

I listened to all their glowing plans and projects and felt my own hopes rise. I had failed to make the world listen to me,—a nobody. With these two, it was different; they were learned men, well known savants whose words were listened to with respect and attention, whose opinions were adopted because they were known to be careful students who did not make a statement for which they could not vouch; men whose books were accepted as the highest educational works in their particular line; men whose conclusions were received as final, who in fact were authorities whom none ventured to question or doubt.

The few days spent together by the two friends must, indeed, have been happy ones to them. It was, as it were, the resting place before launching out into the troubled stormy sea. I am not sure that they ever met again on earth, but their interests were never again divided.

Like myself, they found the world loath to accept the new teachings, and even their names would not carry with them a conviction of the disinterested good-will they bore towards their fellow creatures. They were both indefatigable in their efforts and to the last maintained the cause for which they had sacrificed so much. Someday the universities of Leipzig and Breslau will be proud of owning these two men as the pioneers who went out from their midst to advocate a despised cause, sacrificing much and suffering much, but imbued with the same spirit which animated the early Christians and made them steadfast to the end.

We, in England, where freedom of thought is not only tolerated but encouraged among high and low alike, can scarcely understand the position of men in Lutheran countries, who secede from the etablished church, and presume to hold opinions of their own. They may become Atheists or Materialists, and nobody troubles about it: but they may not advocate any other views concerning the means of salvation than those taught by the Clergy or they are immediately looked upon with suspicion. To promulgate their opinions is a heinous offence, and punishable by severe penalties. Knowing this I can understand that in advocating spiritualism and in endeavouring to teach its grand truths, these men found they had taken on themselves a thankless task. It made them old before their time and cut short their lives.

It was with sorrow I learned a few years, later that Professor Zöllner had earned his crown of martyrdom, and had passed on to the shadowland to wear it. No doubt he was glad to go, but there were many left who missed him from the ranks; many workers in his native country, who felt that in losing his co-operation they were losing a great support. Although he has gone his work remains, and will be valued in the years to come when a later and wiser generation peoples the land he lived in. But at the time I write of, when the friends were rejoicing in their new-found brotherhood they did not know of the trials in store and were content to enjoy to the full the happiness of the hour, never fearing what the future might hold. During the visit of the Professor, the Doctor's rooms were crowded with callers all anxiously enquiring about this new thing. The news had spread like wild-fire throughout scholastic circles and the most extraordinary reports were in circulation. Many imagined that the Doctor kept a supply of ghosts on hand to perform miracles of legerdemain, healing the sick, or giving information about lost friends or property.

"What am I to do with these good people?" he said once in comic despair. "They don't seem to understand that the name spiritualist is not synonymous with that of wizard or dealer in Black Magic." It was indeed difficult to know how to satisfy all enquirers, nor could I help him, my ignorance of German being an effectual barrier between me and non-English speaking visitors. This at first was considered a drawback to my usefulness, but the Doctor often remarked later that he was glad of it, or I should be talked to death if I had to answer all the questions put to me by the strangers who thronged his rooms.

Among the doctor's most intimate friends was a gentleman whom I will here call Herr X. This gentleman enjoyed the reputation of being the strongest man in Silesia, and he was evidently proud of it. He spent much of his time in athletic exercises and frequently boasted to the doctor of some of his feats of strength and was always listened to good-humouredly.

"Strong as you are though," remarked the doctor one day, "I don't believe you could hold down that table, if "Walter" chose to lift it."

"Don't you think so? Well, my dear Sir, if Walter has no objection I'll soon satisfy you on that point; I'd like to see the ghost or the man either, for that matter, that I could not beat if it is a question of strength."

"Suppose we try him," said the doctor to me. "It would do no harm to take the conceit out of this young man."   .

I had no objection, so seated myself at one end of an oblong table, and waited for what might come. To my surprise Heir X. removed his coat, unfastened his wristbands, squared his shoulders, and laid hold of the unoffending table as though it were some unruly animal that required keeping in its place by sheer strength.

Seeing that the table made no attempt to move, all this preparation seemed superfluous and I watched Herr X. with no little curiosity. He held the table down as though he would crush it through the floor. The muscles of his arms were strained to their utmost tension; beads of perspiration stood on his forehead, the veins swelled, and he seemed to be exerting all his strength, but the table did not try to move. Every now and again he would relax his hold for a moment to wipe away the moisture from his brow; and then the table would give little short quick jumps, which instantly caused Herr X. to redouble his efforts and to make a grab at the table, as a cat would pounce on a mouse that was about to escape its clutches.

This went on for something over half an hour, but with the exception of these small signs of life the table remained perfectly passive. At the expiration of that time, Herr X. stood upright and dried his face and neck, remarking that "the spirits knew better than to tackle him."

I felt disappointed and judging from the doctor's expressions he was also feeling some degree of chagrin.

At this juncture the table began to move in a gentle rocking manner, and seeing this Herr X. made a fresh attack, but this time the table kept on its gentle regular movements neither quicker nor slower, neither diverging an inch more to the right nor to the left, in spite of the strength which Herr X. tried to exert. He did his best; he held on as if for his life; he threw himself on the table where he was rocked as in a cradle. The spectacle of this Hercules struggling with a table was so intensely funny, that *I* felt helpless with laughter. At last he gave up in anger.

"It is a down-right swindle." he exclaimed angrily: "it is not fair."

"What is a swindle? What ist't fair" demanded the doctor.

"Why that styie of wrestling, it is all a trick on that Walter's part. He just made me exhaust myself before ever he started, and it is no test of strength. I suppose," he said rather suspiciously, "you think I have been beaten, but I protest against that manner of wrestling. If Walter will play fair I'll guarantee I'll hold the table in spite of him but I wont go in for that style again."

His indignation was so ludicrous that it was with difficulty we could refrain from tormenting him as to the uselessness of his wasted strength.

Herr X. became a spiritualist, not because its teachings appealed to him, not because he was interested in knowing of the existence of another life, but because he found a *table* which had played a trick on him, and made him exhaust his strength before beginning the contest in which he was worsted.

It has often struck me as strange that different temperaments require such different manifestations to make any impression on them. Some men would not consider it worth a thought if all the chairs and tables in the house became animated. Others again would view all the materialised forms that were ever produced, with perfect indifference. Others would look with contempt on all the inspired writings in the world.

The man who cared nothing for all the most beautiful thoughts expressed by our spirit friends, would be overwhelmed with awe and reverence when the movements of a table nearly broke his leg or knocked him into a corner. Another man believed neither the one nor the other, but would have believed that the moon was made of cream cheese when, at his request, a knot was tied in a ring cut from a tanned hide without the ring being cut, broken, or otherwise damaged. At the same time I do not pretend to say that any of these men became spiritualists in the true sense of the word. Belief in phenomena, does not make the believer a spiritualist.

Dr. Friese had no sooner got through the first interviews with his friends after his resignation than he set himself to work with his first book on the subject of spiritualism. It was published in Leipzig under the title "Jenseits des Grabes." Shortly afterwards followed a larger work "Stimmen aus dem Reich der Geister" which owed its origin principally to the writings and communications of Stafford and Walter.

It was with real sorrow we parted, when the time came, to go our different ways; he to continue his studies on the now absorbing subject, and to publish his books; I to return to England to obtain if possible employment for my pencil. During the months of study, under the direction of the doctor, I had made great progress in the art of drawing, or at least I thought I had, and believed I could readily obtain work of a lucrative nature.

I may as well confess at once that I found other people did not express the same opinion, in fact the sketches of which I was most proud elicited the remark, "I suppose this is to be viewed from a distance," from one of my friends whose criticism I had requested.

I felt terribly discouraged at first, and inclined to give up my idea of ever becoming an artist, but other work crowded upon me till I only took up my pencil as an amusement for some years to come. The missionary spirit again took possession of me, and as I had come amongst a number of persons who were also strongly interested in making proselytes, I found many earnest supporters who were ready to help with advice and suggestions.

CHAPTER XVI.

NEW MANIFESTATIONS.

"There is mystery in all things and in all beings;—in star and atom—in ocean and dew-drop—in tree and flower—in animal and worm—in man and angel in Bible and God! Not a world exists in which there is not mystery."

Dr. Davies

A CIRCLE was formed of from twelve to fifteen persons, my old friends Mr. and Mrs. F. being of the number, together with one or two others who had assisted in the first of our experiments. For the convenience of the different members whose homes were situated in various parts of the town, it was decided to use my painting-room or studio as a séance room, it being easy of access to all, and here we met twice a week for the purpose of experimenting.

We were most desirous of cultivating the portrait-sketching, as I felt myself now much more proficient in the art, and even had the belief that under favorable conditions I could succeed in making colored sketches. This I attempted on one or two occasions and was fairly successful, but the power to see the spirits in the distinct clear manner necessary for this, was intermittent and we were frequently disappointed. Sometimes, indeed, success attended us and the portraits obtained were invariably recognized. Several of these were afterwards photographed, but the originals were kept by the friends who claimed them as the portraits of their lost relatives. I have frequently regretted that any of them passed out of my hands before having them photographed, as I only retain the very few originals which were not claimed. As it is they are scattered far and wide in different parts of the world.

Another experiment was to read closed or sealed letters. The first attempt was fairly successful. I could see the writing distinctly, but had to follow the folds of the paper, turning it over and over to trace the lines. It was enclosed in seven envelopes, gummed, and sealed, and was written in a language I did not know, so that I had to spell every word aloud in order that a member of the circle should write it according to my dictation.

Another time a letter was given me to read, but in spite of repeated trials, I was unable to make anything of it. At last, once when I took up the envelope I was delighted to find its contents clearly visible to me, but it also was in a foreign language—Swedish—and I was compelled to copy each word carefully, not knowing its meaning.

At the first I used to wait anxiously for the letters to be opened, to be assured that I really had seen the actual writing, but as there had never been a mistake so far, I had no more fear; I knew I had seen what was behind the sealed cover.

Even this power fluctuated. Given two letters to read, the one would be as clear and distinct as though spread out before me, the other perfectly impenetrable. Once or twice I have kept such letters by me, trying now and again to decipher the sealed contents. In some cases after having kept them for awhile I was enabled to see and read them, though with difficulty, having to guess at the words very often. Frequently the paper appeared of a murky tone, sometimes quite black, and the written words indistinguishable. Strange to say, I always had a particular aversion to such letters, in some cases almost amounting to horror. I hated to touch them, and after having done so I felt an instinctive desire to wash my hands. Quite in vain I tried to combat this feeling as it interfered frequently with my usefulness.

Any compulsion which I put on myself was, however, detrimental to the exercise of these powers. Many times I have said to myself "I will read this letter and win him over to our cause," not because I had any particular sympathy for or with the writer, but perhaps because his social or influential position made him a desirable partisan, or because his obstinate unbelief excited a feeling of antagonism, and I was anxious to show I was right in my assertions that it could be done. I do not remember, however, ever meeting with any marked success in such a case. At other times letters from perfect strangers, whom I had never seen, were clear as crystal to my vision.

This power, although affording our circle a good deal of entertainment, when confined to ourselves, gave rise to considerable disagreableness, when it became talked about among outsiders, and more than once we were annoyed by the comments of persons of anti-spiritualistic proclivities who did not hesitate to say it was all an imposition. It was most difficult to keep these things entirely within the select circle we had formed, although such had been our first intention. People were constantly begging the acquaintanceship of one or the other of us, and by this means gaining admission to our seances. Indeed the friendship of many whom I most highly esteem dates from that time, and of course I have also a distinct memory of some who were not friends. At least I never counted them as such till one day just lately I was told by Stafford, that "Enemies are often of more value than friends, inasmuch as they discover our faults and magnify them, hide or ignore our virtues, and by so doing show us clearly the need of improvement. Friends, on the contrary, magnify our virtues and ignore our faults."

I suppose this is all very true, but I think most people prefer friends to enemies, though enemies may be necessary as correctives occasionally, as were the doses of rhubarb and magnesia, or the fever-powders of my childhood. But I did not like the medicine then; neither do I value enemies now, in spite of the wise sayings of Stafford. I have no objection to anti-spiritualists, in fact I enjoy converting one of them, but I do I object to the man who denounces a thing he does not understand, and of which he has no personal experience. I consider it arrogant assumption in the man who without experience or knowledge attempts to question the faith of those who have spent a life-time in careful research and experiment, no matter what the object may have been. In respect to this particular subject it is only the utterly ignorant who would so presume. The man who has spent even a little time in unprejudiced enquiry would not dare to say: "There is nothing in it." He might find much that annoyed him, much which did' not appeal to him, but he would be silenced. He would only say: "I do not understand it."

At the time of which I write, 1873 to 1880, there was a good deal of excited feeling with respect to the phenomena. There were several mediums, whose séances were reported in various papers, and the anti-spiritualists took the opportunity to make hay while the sun shone. The most ignorant men who knew how to string words together stood up on the public platforms and denounced spiritualism with all the force of which they were capable. Following the advice of a celebrated barrister to a younger colleague, when they saw the case going against them, they abused their opponent with every invective and opprobrious epithet in their vocabulary. Possibly these men were the enemies, who, Stafford would say, were of value, but they certainly made the work of mediums very difficult just at that time.

One of the mediums who came in for a good deal of abuse from these wise lecturers was Mrs. M., a young married lady with whom I had some slight acquaintance for a considerable time, and whose seances for materialisation I had more than once attended. She had previously used the room which I now- occupied and her cabinet still remained in the corner. Her health was not very good at the time, and she had discontinued her seances. One evening we had been holding our usual weekly meeting which had proved quite unsuccessful, probably owing to a storm of wind and rain which made the prospect of the journey home very unenviable. We closed our meeting early and waited till the rain should cease before going out. In the meantime someone proposed that one of us should seat himself behind the curtains of Mrs. M.'s cabinet and see if a materialised ghost would present itself. As no one had any objection, this was done and we seated ourselves round about and began to sing. We sang every tune we knew of, and were beginning to wonder how long this was to last, when the sound of a snore from behind the curtains announced the fact that our "medium" was having a more comfortable time than we outside, and we declined to continue to produce soporific melodies for his benefit, and therefore requested him to • give up his place to some less sleepy person. Thereupon he took his seat in the circle, and Mrs. F. volunteered to take the vacated chair behind the curtains. We began to sing as before, making it a condition, however, that she was not to go to sleep and keep us singing to no purpose. Less than five minutes elapsed, however, before Mrs. F. rushed out declaring there was something alive in the cabinet and she was afraid. This we looked on as only an excuse; so we opened the curtains and examined the interior of the small square cabinet. There was no sign of anything living or dead, nothing indeed but a wooden chair!

We persuaded her to try again, and she very reluctantly resumed her seat, while we ranged ourselves as before and began a new tune—or scarcely began, however, before Mrs. F. sprang out declaring that nothing would induce her to remain a moment longer behind the curtains, as she was certain there was something alive there. Finding persuasion useless I boldly declared my intention of braving the "something alive" and seated myself in the cabinet while Mrs. F. took my place in the circle.

For a few minutes there was perfect stillness, and I was beginning to think that my friend's imagination was very strong, when I became conscious of a curious disturbance of the air within the enclosure. There was no sound, and as the thick curtains effectually excluded the light I could see nothing, but the air around me seemed agitated as though a bird was fluttering about.

I would not confess it even to myself, but at that moment I felt something very like fear, and a desire to rush out into the light and company of the singers; but I sat still; in fact I felt glued to my chair, dreading that the "something" would touch me, and having the conviction that if it did I should scream. I turned hot and cold by turns, and would have given much to have been on the I other side of the curtains. I knew I had only to stretch out my hand and draw them aside, but there was in some way an indescribable sensation of isolation and loneliness which seemed to place me at an immeasurable distance from the others. This curious feeling was almost mastering my desire to be brave, and I was about to make a rush into the room, when a hand was placed on my shoulder, pressing me down upon my chair from which I had risen.

Strangely enough this touch, which under ordinary circumstances would have startled me beyond measure, had the effect of soothing my fear and excitement. I remembered how one stormy night long ago when watching in an agony of fear beside my sleeping brothers and sister, a hand was placed on my arm; now as then the pressure of the unseen fingers acted like magic and I was no longer afraid.

The fluttering sensation in the air ceased and all was still. The hand was lifted and now enquiries came from the sitters who began to weary of their self-imposed task of singing.

"Do you see anything in there?"

"Have you found something alive?"

"How long are we to sit like this. Let us give it up; it's not raining now, we can go home."

"Well,"—as I came from behind the curtains, "did you feel or see anything curious?"

"I saw nothing, but felt a strange vibratory movement as though a bird was flying and once something touched my shoulder."

This circumstance was the subject of discussion for the next few days, and on the occasion of our next séance, which also happened to be finished earlier than usual, I was requested to make another trial with the cabinet, whereupon I took my place as on the previous occasion. The cabinet, I must explain, was simply a small recess in one corner of the room, the front hung by thick red baize curtains from the ceiling to the floor. During séances the room was dimly lighted by one or two gas jets which were generally turned low, but which sufficiently illuminated the room to enable anyone in it to see and observe all that took place, and to read or make notes, but not sufficient to penetrate the thickness of the curtains; so that I, sitting behind them, was comparatively speaking in absolute darkness, while those on the other side had sufficient light for all ordinary purposes.

It was not long before the same strange disturbances in the air began as on the previous occasion. I felt my hair blown and lifted by currents of air, and cool breezes played about my face and hands. Then began a strange sensation, which I had sometimes felt at seances. Frequently I have heard it described by others as of cobwebs being passed over the face, but to me, who watched it curiously, it seemed that I could feel fine threads being drawn out of the pores of my skin.

I experienced none of the fear of the previous evening. At first I had a strange eerie feeling somewhat akin to it, but that passed off, and I became perfectly calm and indisposed to move, or to answer any of the many questions addressed to me by my friends outside. At the same time I took a great interest in analysing my own sensations and wondered as to what would come of the experiment, for that something was about to happen I was certain.

"There is a man's face!" I heard a voice exclaim.

"Dear me, so there is. Goodness! how queer."

"Can you see it?"

"Yes, we can all see it. Who can it be?"

"Where is it?" I asked, roused by these exclamations.

"There, between the curtains. A round face with dark eyebrows, hair, and moustache. There! he is nodding and laughing. Can't you see him?"

It was in vain I strained my eyes. I could see nothing. A tiny gleam of light through the opening of the curtains would seem to indicate that something was holding them back, at about the height of a man's head from the floor, but that was all.

"Dear me! I wonder who he is." "What a nice face he has." "Can you see his teeth, when he smiles?" "See how he nods, when we speak."

These and similar ejaculations excited my curiosity, so that I made a move to go outside the curtains and have a look at the mysterious visitor. When I stood up my knees felt strangely weak, and I wondered if I were not very well. I put my head out at the side of the curtain and looked as directed towards the centre opening and there gazing down on me with merry laughing eyes was the face of Walter! I recognised him instantly, as he appeared with the light from the gas jet falling full on his face; just the same features as I had seen and sketched under such very different conditions.

"Walter!" I exclaimed. He nodded and smiled.

I felt weak, I was astonished, and there was a sensation of something else which I could not understand, so that I sank powerless into my seat again.

Then began a volley of questions to Walter, who evidently replied by sufficiently expressive gestures, which however I could not see. But I gathered that Walter was highly delighted with his evening's work.

———

CHAPTER XVII.

MATERIALISED SPIRITS.

"From the misty land, that belongs
To the vast unknown."
LONGFELLOW

THE result of our evening's work was the subject of eager congratulation among the members of our circle, who prophesied
great things if we only continued to pursue our experiments in
the same direction. For myself, I cannot say that I felt anything
but the natural curiosity and interest which such a phenomenon
would excite. I had seen materialised spirits at other séances, but
to tell the truth I had not been particularly struck with anything
I had experienced in that line so far. I will not say that I disbe-
lieved in the genuineness of the manifestations, although on one
or two occasions I had great difficulty in disabusing my mind of
the conviction that it was the form of the medium which posed
as that of the spirit. In fact this phase of manifestation did not
appeal to me, and I felt that in cultivating it I should to some
extent in some way or other be degrading or debasing the power
I possessed. It was a long time before I could see the matter in
the light in which my friends represented it to me. That all manifestations are equally valuable and worthy of cultivation,—that
every fact that can be indubitably established is of incalculable
value in building up a science,—that this particular phase of
phenomena was the one on which many hopes were built for
the establishment of the truths which spiritualists claimed, as
proving the reality of another state of existence and the existence
of a link between it and our world;—many such arguments were
brought to bear on me, and though I could not see the immense
value of these manifestations above others, I had no desire to run
counter to the wishes of my friends and consented at last with
reluctance to continue the experiments.

Medium and materialised spirit photographed together.
The medium shielding her eyes from the effect
of the magnesium light.
(Copied from a photo June 1890).

Medium and materialised spirit photographed together,
a few seconds after the foregoing.
The spirit covered the medium with drapery which the
light apparently dissolved.

When I had previously attended séances for materialisation, whatever my private opinion had been of their origin I kept it to myself: but others of my acquaintance were not so reticent nor did they hesitate at times to make remarks, anything but commendatory to the spirits or medium, so that it annoyed me to think I might probably expose myself to the same insults.

Here however an old friend, Mr. A., who had formed one of our first circle, stepped in, and to prevent any unpleasantness of that kind proposed that we should work on different lines. We would carefully pick out those of our friends who were interested in cultivating this class of manifestation, and invite them to join a bi-weekly meeting, but only on the condition that nothing that passed should be made public until the expiration of a series of twelve seances; that during this time each should bind him or herself to attend regularly and punctually, no excuse being accepted for non-attendance except that of ill-health; and that no strangers were to be admitted under any circumstances.

These invitations and conditions were sent to some fifteen or twenty friends and were accepted, I agreeing to do all in my power to fulfil my part. I was quite willing to give the matter a six weeks' trial, thinking that by the end of that time we should have seen whether or not there was anything to be gained by prosecuting this phase of experiment. I felt that I owed my friends some consideration, as they had followed patiently the various developments which had attended our investigations some of which I think must have tired them terribly. In spite of my feeling of repugnance to the phenomena which we were about to cultivate I thought that by giving six weeks' for the purpose of gratifying my friends I was repaying them to some extent for the help they had accorded me on the road to spiritual knowledge, which I could scarcely have reached had it not been for their kind co-operation. These then were the motives which actuated me in the new departure we were about to make.

The séances began. The cabinet was a new, lightly constructed one, of about three feet in depth, nearly nine feet long, and over six feet high. The length was, however, divided by two gauze partitions, making thus three divisions, each about three feet square, open only to the front which was hung by thick dark curtains. The idea of a cabinet of this shape and size was partly Mr. A's, and arose out of consideration for my dislike of coming into immediate contact with the "materialised ghosts" and partly to see whether the gauze would offer any impediment to the coming and going of the forms. There were no means of entrance nor exit except by the front, neither could any person in one compartment get into either of the other two without breaking the gauze partition, or going out by the curtains and entering from the front. The whole arrangement was extremely simple and, so far as I am aware, the most satisfactory of any so-called test cabinets that have been tried, giving the medium perfect freedom while insuring the others from the possibility of supposing that they are the victims of vulgar trickery.

I have very strong and definite opinions of all "tests" and of people who advocate them, but these opinions have been the growth of time and bitter experience. At the beginning of our experiments I had everything to learn and like others had to begin with the A. B C.

No one had ever presumed to cast a doubt on my integrity. I had always worked from pure interest in the subject, and watched each development with quite as much, if not more, interest than any of my friends. These strange powers which unfolded themselves one after another delighted as well as mystified me, and I criticised myself and tried to analyse them impartially. If I could have developed these strange faculties by myself it would have given me greater satisfaction as I could, I thought, understand the workings and *modus operandi* of evolvement better when not distracted by hearing the conjectures, suppositions and theories of others: but this I could not do. Alone I was comparatively powerless. I sometimes looked upon my good friends as necessary evils, rather than assistants, and had I been able to prosecute my experiments alone, I should at this juncture have infinitely preferred it, but this being impossible the tests proposed were just as much to my taste as to theirs. As long as they were applied simply to watch the result I was as eager as anyone to suggest fresh schemes in order to see how the spirits would act when hindrances were placed in their way.

The room was arranged so as to give the greatest facilities for both sitters and spirits. The windows, which were opposite the cabinet, were partially darkened, the daylight being admitted through the upper parts which were coloured red or orange, and which could be made to admit more or less light as required. This was for daylight séances. For the evening a clever arrangement of gas lighting was devised. The end walls of the room were covered by a screen of red or orange-coloured paper, placed some inches from the wall. Behind this screen, a gas pipe was placed, running horizontally the length of the wall, and in this pipe were several jets of gas, which could be regulated by a tap outside. This tap was manipulated either by the spirits themselves or by one of the sitters. The light from several small jets of gas being thus dispersed by the tinted paper made a sufficient, as well as a very agreable, light, each part of the room being equally illuminated, either with a bright or a dim light as might be required. Within the cabinet, however, black darkness reigned, unless the curtains at one or the other of the compartments were raised, when any-one seated within it could see distinctly to the opposite end, the gauze partitions offering no obstacle to the eye, although impenetrable to the body. The room was warmed by an asbestos fire when necessary, and presented on the whole, a cheerful comfortable aspect.

Having completed the number of guests who were to form our circle, each one having declared him or herself willing to assist as far as able and to accept the conditions laid down, we began our fresh course of study, full of interest and expectation for what might result. Mr. A. was to be general manager. Mr. F. undertook to keep notes of every circumstance, every detail as it occurred. Mrs. B., a pianist, took upon herself to conduct the singing, in which up to the present we had not indulged to any extent. We had a small organ in the room, and this lady took great pains to improve the singing of our friends and make it a pleasure rather than a torment to us. Another gentleman stipulated that we should begin our evening's experiments with a prayer to God for guidance, and for deliverance from evil powers.

The expense of all the arrangements in our seance room was covered by the members of the circle who subscribed to a fund for the purpose. The surplus, after providing for the small current expenses, such as gas and rent was devoted to helping the poorer of the sick persons who thronged around us for assistance.

Never in my life before had I suspected the want, misery, and sickness which existed in the world, nor how little doctors could do to alleviate it; how in spite of all efforts made by the charitable and kind-hearted benefactors in our midst such wretchedness could exist. I turned absolutely sick sometimes, when standing face to face with the horrors of disease and want, which I felt how powerless I was to help. Many times have I asked myself, when visiting some den of squalor and misery, "Can this be God's world; can these be his children? Of what use to give medicine to these pale emaciated little ones, who were starving for sunlight and fresh air or for nourishing food, whose limbs refused to carry the wasted forms, a consequence of their parents' weakness or culpability, inheriting disease from them as their only birth-right?" I have wondered often, if I had made a world and peopled it with such a result, whether I would not have done as I used to do with a faulty drawing—destroy it and begin afresh. It seemed to me that there was no mercy in helping these poor miserable victims of ignorance and disease, to prolong a wretched existence. But Stafford thought differently. He was indefatigable in his efforts to assist in mitigating the suffering; never wearied in advising, teaching, exhorting, diving at once to the root of the evil, pointing out where mistakes had been made, and how to remedy them if not too late.

He never hesitated in pointing out, and rebuking in scathing words, diseases caused, not by ignorance, but by deliberate infraction of the laws of Nature. His sympathy with suffering was as unbounded as his wish to help; consequently there was no lack of objects on which to expend any surplus funds. Medicines he objected to, on the ground that drugs only set up another disease, in many cases as harmful as the one to be cured. His methods of remedy were chiefly, a more natural way of living, simple diet, fresh air, physical exercise, and a knowledge of right and wrong to enable the sick person to cure himself. "Give the children food," he would write sometimes, "and let drugs alone." So that the medicines carried into some of the courts and alleys of the slums were more frequently in the shape of oat-meal, bread, fruit and similar comestibles, than in unpalatable mixtures from the chemists. My clientelle rapidly increased till I never knew what it was to have an hour to myself, in spite of the help I received from Mr. and Mrs. F., which was not a little. In fact had it not been for them, much of the work would never have been accomplished.

Stafford, although not saying much, contrived to let me understand that he did not place much value on the experiments we were about to make and this disappointed me, but I hoped for his co-operation later.

At the first few séances the sitters in the room declared they saw the curtains of the different compartments open and faces look out of them; but I saw nothing. One of these faces Mrs. F. recognised as that of Walter, and she asked him if he would not come out and show himself fully to the company. He replied by raps or signals, the manner of which I have forgotten, that he would gladly do so, but that he had no clothes and did not wish to shock the ladies by appearing in the costume of the garden of Eden.

"We will lend you some garments" said a gentleman but Walter declined.

Mrs. F. then asked if Walter would like her to make him some clothes and, if she did so, would he wear them and leave the shelter of the cabinet at our next meeting? Whether Walter signified acceptance of the offer or not I am not sure, but during the next few days Mrs. F. and I busied ourselves in fashioning a garment which we intended to place at Walter's disposal at our next meeting. We chose white muslin as being more "spiritual" than any other material; we cut and planned, stitched and hemmed, and finally viewed our handiwork with great satisfaction. We had made a sort of dressing-gown with voluminous folds and wide open sleeves, getting our ideas of its suitability from the pictures of the costumes of the saints and angels. This garment we carried to the seance room and proudly exhibited it to the rest of the company, and then placed it within the middle compartment of the cabinet, to be in readiness for Walter when he came. When he did come, however, the first intimation of his presence was the rolling up of the garment we had made with so much care, and the handing it over to Mrs. F. with the message that it was not suitable nor required. And I Walter himself stepped boldly out from the cabinet into the midst of the circle, dressed in garments which, in whitness, softness, and fineness put our gift to shame.

Walter was evidently very much elated at his success in "making a new body for himself" as he termed it, as well as his cleverness in providing the draperies which elicited so much admiration. He seemed to make himself rapidly familiar with all the company, and their conversation and remarks excited no little curiosity in me, for during all the time I was seated in the darkness of the cabinet, unable to see a glimpse of what was going on outside. In spite of my wish to take part in the doings on the other side of the curtain, I felt strangely inert and listless; not sleepy; indeed, my brain seemed more wide awake and active than I had ever known it. Thoughts, impressions, chased themselves with lightening like rapidity, sounds which I knew to be at a distance were as though close to my ears; I felt conscious of the thoughts, or rather the feelings, of every one in the room, but had no inclination to as much as lift a finger to enable me to see anything, although at the same time burning with curiosity to catch a sight of Walter walking about in their midst.

Later on I discovered that this was not merely listlessness or inertia, but that I had literally no strength to exert myself without making a great effort, which invariably compelled the materialised forms to retire to the cabinet as though deprived of the power to stand or support themselves, but *this fact*, as well as many others, *was not to be learned without pain.*

———————

CHAPTER XVIII.

"YOLANDE."

"What is't?   A Spirit
Lord, how it looks about!   Believe me sir,
It carries a brave form:— but 'tis a spirit"
THE TEMPEST, *scene II*

BEFORE the close of the series of séances, we had progressed so far that Walter was able, apparently without difficulty, to appear in our midst, evidently as solid and material in body as one of ourselves. He would frequently describe in writing some other spirits who were present though invisible to us, unable to perform the work of clothing themselves with material as he had done. This evidently suggested to Walter the idea of acting the part of valet to these less clever ones, and assisting them in the work of materialising. After this conclusion on his part we saw little of Walter, but scarcely an evening passed that two or more strange forms did not pay us a visit. Among them was one who appeared to quickly become independent of Walter's helpful offices. This was "Yolande," a young Arab girl of fifteen or sixteen years, according to Walters statements who soon became, as it were, the leading feature of our séances; a slender olive-skinned maiden whose naivete and gracefulness made her the wonder and admiration of the circle.

The first time she made her appearance among us, her curiosity and inquisitiveness seemed unbounded. Everything she saw interested her deeply, from the dresses of the company to the furniture of the room. The organ was her special delight, and she was quick in imitating the melodies which Mrs. B. played for her, though she was never able to manage the bellows of which, apparently she could not understand the use. One of the gentlemen, a detective in the police force, possessed a silver cornet on which he was an accomplished performer, and on noticing Yolande's love for music, he one evening brought it with him, and played for her some of the tunes she liked. He had some arrangement by which the sound of the otherwise loud notes was softened to a sweet mellowness that was not out of place in the room.

Yolande had seated herself on the floor to listen to this wonder. When Mr. J. had played a tune, Yolande begged to have the instrument which she examined with great care. Every part of it was inspected minutely, and when this was done she tried to play upon it. She failed, however, in producing a sound, although she tried both ends, and at last gave up the attempt in evident disappointment.

Someone had given her some small silver bells, which pleased her mightily. They were strung on a tape, and she frequently put them round her ankles or her wrists, and when Mr. J. played on his cornet Yolande kept time to the tune by movements of her graceful feet or arms, producing an admirable accompaniment with the sound of the tinkling bells. This performance seemed to her a great delight, and it became a matter of wonder how she could, by her clever movements, alter the sound of the bells to suit the melody that was being played. Sometimes they would ring out in a slow soft sleepy manner like trickling water-drops heard in the distance, then quick and clear like the rippling notes of a song-bird; and again like castanets played by a proficient hand, her body and arms waving gracefully the while, as she sat on the floor or stood in the centre of the circle.

For most of the descriptions of Yolande's many charms I am indebted to the members of the circle, and to minutes from the notes kept by Mr. F., because, though I was as it were, all ears, my necessary position within the cabinet deprived me of the use of my eyes during the seances. It seemed to me that the "spirits" rather avoided me, at any rate they never appeared to consider it necessary to gratify my very natural curiosity when anything called for more attention or wonder than usual.

Once I saw Yolande very distinctly, but I believe it was more by accident than by design on her part. She had been amusing herself outside for some time, and opened the curtains of the next compartment to where I sat, with the evident intention of entering, but something called her attention and she stood holding back both curtains, the light falling full upon her face and form, the gas-lighted room enabling me to make a careful survey of her figure. Her thin draperies allowed the rich olive tint of her neck, shoulders, arms, and ankles to be plainly visible. The long black waving hair hung over her shoulders to below her waist and was confined by a small turban-shaped headdress. Her features were small, straight, and piquant; the eyes were dark, large, and lively; her every movement was as full of grace as those of a young child, or, as it struck me then when I saw her standing half shyly, half boldly, between the curtains, like a young roe-deer.

Yolande soon became remarkably clever. Her fearless activity, childlike curiosity, and wonder over every new thing that came under her observation, were a source of constant interest to us all. She had a great love for bright colors and glittering objects, examining with the utmost attention any trinkets which the ladies wore, sometimes adorning herself with them, and appearing to derive immense satisfaction from the admiring remarks of the circle. A lady once brought a brilliantly colored Persian silk scarf, which Yolande regarded with great delight, and immediately draped about her shoulders and waist. This scarf she could not be induced to part with. When she had disappeared and the seance closed a careful search was made, but it was not to be found. The next time she came, the lady asked her what she had done with it. Yolande seemed a little non-plussed at the question, but in an instant she made a few movements with her hands in the air and over her shoulders, and the scarf was there, draped as she had arranged it on the previous evening. How it came, where it came from, no one saw. Yolande stood before them without it, robed in the soft white spirit-garments which scarcely concealed her graceful form; yet, a movement of her slender brown hand, and the bare shoulders were covered with the brightly colored folds of the silken shawl. She never trusted this scarf out of her hands. When sometimes she herself gradually dissolved into mist under the scrutiny of twenty pairs of eyes, the shawl was left lying on the floor we would say, "At last she has forgotten it"; but no, the shawl would itself gradually vanish in the same manner as its wearer and no search which we might afterwards make ever discovered its whereabouts. Yet Yolande assured us gleefully that we failed to see it only because we were blind, for the shawl never left the room. This seemed to amuse her, and she was never tired of mystifying us by making things invisible to our eyes or by introducing into the room flowers which had not been brought by human hands.

One of the members of the circle giving an account at the time of this wonderful creature, describes her strange appearances and disappearances in the following words:—

"First a filmy, cloudy, patch of something white is observed on the floor, in front of the cabinet. It then gradually expands, visibly extending itself as if it were an animated patch of muslin, lying fold upon fold, on the floor, until extending about two and a half by three feet and having a depth of a few inches—perhaps six or more. Presently it begins to rise slowly in or near the centre, as if a human head were underneath it, while the cloudy film on the floor begins to look more like muslin falling into folds about the portion so mysteriously rising. By the time it has attained two or more feet, it looks as if a child were under it and moving its arms about in all directions as if manipulating something underneath.

"It continues rising, oftentimes sinking somewhat to rise again higher than before, until it attains a height of about five feet, when its form can be seen as if arranging the folds of drapery about its figure.

"Presently the arms rise considerably above the head and open outwards through a mass of cloud like spirit drapery, and Yolande stands before us unveiled, graceful and beautiful, nearly five feet in height, having a turban-like head-dress, from beneath which her long black hair hangs over her shoulders and down her back.

"Her body dress, of Eastern form, displays every limb and contour of the body, while the superflous white veil-like drapery is wrapped round her for convenience, or thrown down on the carpet out of the way till required again.

"All this occupies from ten to fifteen minutes to accomplish.

"When she disappears or dematerialises it is as follows:—
"Stepping forward to show herself and be identified by any strangers then present, she slowly and deliberately opens out the veil-like superfluous drapery; expanding it she places it over her head, and spreads it around her like a great bridal veil, and then immediately but slowly sinks down, becoming less bulky as she collapses, dematerialising her body beneath the cloud-like drapery until it has little or no resemblance to Yolande. Then she further collapses until she has no resemblance to a human form, and more rapidly sinks down to fifteen or twelve inches. Then suddenly the form falls into a heaped patch of drapery—literally Yolande's left-off clothing which slowly but visibly melts into nothingness.

"The dematerialising of Yolande's body occupies from two to five minutes, while the disappearance of the drapery occupies from a half to two minutes. On one occasion, however, she did not dematerialise this drapery or veil, but left the whole lying on the carpet in a heap, until another spirit came out of the cabinet to look at it for a moment, as if moralising on poor Yolande's disappearance. This taller spirit also disappeared and was replaced by the little brisk vivacious child form of Ninia, the Spanish girl, who likewise came to look at Yolande's remains; and curiously picking up the left off garments, proceeded to wrap them round her own little body, which was already well clothed with drapery."

Once Yolande stepped out of the cabinet and came just by me, having her veil over her head, and playfully peeping towards another part of the cabinet in evident expectation of somebody coming. Presently the curtains opened and another taller form came forward into full view of us all. It was amusing to see Yolande's impatience at the delay in emerging from the cabinet, which she expressed by stamping her bare feet on the floor.

Another of these mysterious visitants was one whose name we were told was Y-Ay-Ali, one of the most perfectly beautiful creatures the mind can conceive, her tall stately form and dazzling fairness, majestic bearing and graceful movements, being a distinct contrast to Yolande's kitten-like gestures. Y-Ay-Ali was indeed a creature from a higher world. She came only once or twice visibly, though we were told frequently that she was present; but no one who ever saw her is likely to forget her.

She was evidently one in authority, a teacher for whom Yolande exhibited a loving respect and veneration. We were told that it was she who, though unseen by us, assisted in the production of the magnificent flowers which were so mysteriously brought into our midst.

———————

CHAPTER XIX.

THE IXORA CROCATA.

"Then said the Lord, Thou hast had pity on the gourd, for the which thou hast not labored, neither madest it grow; which came up in a night and perished in a night."

JONAH CH. 4. V. 10

ON ONE occasion I received a letter from a well-known gentleman in Manchester, Mr. W. Oxley, as well as from two equally well-known persons in Germany, asking permission to be present at one of our seances. I laid their requests before the rest of our members and asked them to decide, with the result that all three strangers were present at the next following séance. This seance turned out to be one of extraordinary interest, if indeed one may say that any one of these strange things is more extraordinary than the other; but the circumstance has been published so often in different countries that at least some people have thought it specially worthy of mention.

Mr. Oxley told us he had come with a special object in view, but of which he would not speak unless he gained it; also that the spirits, through another medium, had told him he would succeed in his object, if he could obtain admission to our private circle. We naturally wondered what his object was, and there was some little fear expressed that we, by allowing the other two strangers to be present, might cause the purpose to be frustrated. Just then, too, a slip on descending the stairs had caused me to hurt my arm, putting the elbow out of joint, an accident which was not likely to increase our probabilities of success; so that I went to the séance-room that evening feeling very much inclined to propose putting off the experiment; but on arriving and learning that our visitors' time was extremely limited I decided to try.

We took our accustomed places. Mrs. B. played a solo on the organ and silence reigned, when the curtains of the middle compartment of the cabinet were drawn aside and Yolande stepped out into the room. She glanced inquisitively at the strangers who returned her gaze with interest, evidently admiring the lithe graceful form and the dark eyes of our little Arabian.

One of the circle discribes what followed and I repeat it here for the same reason as I have mentioned elsewhere, that I was not an eye- but a an ear-witness:—

"Yolande crossed the room to where Mr. Reimers sat, a gentleman well known throughout Europe as a prominent spiritualist, and beckoned him to go nearer the cabinet and witness some preparations she was about to make. Here it is as well to say that on previous occasions when Yolande had produced flowers for us, she had given us to understand that sand and water were necessary for the purpose, consequently a supply of fine clean white sand and plenty of water were kept in readiness for possible contingences. When Yolande, accompanied by Mr. Reimers, came to the centre of the circle, she signified her wish for sand and water, and making Mr. R. kneel down on the floor beside her, she directed him to pour sand into the water-carafe, which he did until it was about half full. Then he was instructed to pour in water. This was done, and then by her direction he shook it well and handed it back to her.

"Yolande, after scrutinizing it carefully, placed it on the floor, covering it lightly with the drapery which she took from her shoulders. She then retired to the cabinet, from which she returned once or twice at short intervals as though to see how it was getting on.

"In the meantime Mr. Armstrong had carried away the superfluous water and sand, leaving the carafe standing on the middle of the floor covered by the thin veil, which however did not in the least conceal its shape, the ring or top edge being especially visible.

"We were directed by raps on the floor to sing, in order to harmonise our thoughts, and to take off the edge as it were of the curiosity we were all more or less feeling.

"While we were singing we observed the drapery to be rising from the rim of the carafe. This was perfectly patent to every one of the twenty witnesses watching it closely.

"Yolande came out again from the cabinet and regarded it anxiously. She appeared to examine it carefully, and partially supported the drapery as though afraid of its crushing some tender object underneath. Finally she raised it altogether, exposing to our astonished gaze a perfect plant, of what appeared to be a kind of laurel.

"Yolande raised the carafe, in which the plant seemed to have firmly grown; its roots visible through the glass, being closely packed in the sand.

"She regarded it with evident pride and pleasure and, carrying it in both her hands, crossed the room and presented it to Mr. Oxley, one of the strangers who were present, the Mr. Oxley who is so well known by his philosophical writings on spiritual subjects, and the pyramids of Egypt.

"He received the carafe with the plant, and Yolande retired as though she had completed her task. After examining the plant Mr Oxley, for convenience sake, placed it on the floor beside him, there being no table near at hand. Many questions were asked and curiosity ran high. The plant resembled a large-leafed laurel with dark glossy leaves, but without any blossom. No one present recognized the plant or could assign it to any known species.

"We were called to order by raps, and were told not to discuss the matter but to sing something and then be quiet. We obeyed the command, and after singing, more raps told us to examine the plant anew, which we were only too delighted to do. To our great surprise we then observed that a large circular head of bloom, forming a flower fully five inches in diameter, had opened itself, while standing on the floor at Mr Oxley's feet.

"The flower was of a beautiful orange pink color, or perhaps I might say that salmon color would be a nearer description, for I have never seen the same tints and it is difficult to describe shades of color in words.

Ixora Crocata produced for Mr. William Oxley of
Manchester at a séance held 4 August 1880.
(from a photograph).

"The head was composed of some hundred and fifty of four-star corollas projecting considerably from the stem. The plant was twenty two inches in height, having a thick woody stem which filled the neck of the water carafe. It had twenty nine leaves, averaging from two to two and a half inches in breadth to seven and a half inches at its greatest length. Each leaf was smooth and glossy, resembling at the first glance the laurel which we had at first supposed it to be. The fibrous roots appeared to be growing naturally in the sand.

"We afterwards photographed the plant in the water-bottle, from which by the way it was found imposible to remove it, the neck being much too small to allow the roots to pass; indeed the comparatively slender stem entirely filled the orifice.

"The name we learned was 'Ixora Crocata' and the plant a native of India.

How did the plant come there? Did it grow in the bottle? Had it been brought from India in a dematerialised state and rematerialised in the seance-room?

These were questions which we put to one another without result. We got no satisfactory explanation. Yolande either could not or would not tell us. As far as we could judge,—and the opinion of a professional gardener corroborated our own,—the plant had evidently some years of growth.

"We could see where other leaves had grown and fallen off, and wound-marks which seemed to have healed and grown over long ago. But there was every evidence to show that the plant had grown in the sand in the bottle as the roots were naturally wound around the inner surface of the glass, all the fibres perfect and unbroken as though they had germinated on the spot and had apparently never been disturbed. It had not been thrust into the bottle for the simple reason that it was impossible to pass the large fibrous roots and lower part of the stem through the neck of the bottle, which had to be broken in order to take out the plant."

Mr Oxley in his account which was afterwards published says "I had the plant photographed next morning and afterwards brought it home and placed it in my conservatory under the gardener's care. It lived for three months, when it shrivelled up. I kept the leaves, giving most of them away except the flower and the three top-leaves which the gardener cut off when he took charge of the plant and these I have yet preserved under glass, but they show no signs of dematerialising as yet. Previous to the creation or materialisation of this wonderful plant, the 'Ixora Crocata,' Yolande brought me a rose with a short stem not more than an inch long which I put into my bosom. Feeling something was transpiring, I drew it out and found there were two roses. I then replaced them, and withdrawing them at the conclusion of the meeting, to my astonishment the stem had elongated to seven inches with three full blown roses and a bud upon it with several thorns. These I brought home and kept till they faded, the leaves dropped off and the stem dried up, a proof of their materiality and actuality."

This was only one of Yolande's clever feats but will serve to show how intensely interesting the manifestations were which attended our experiments. Mr Oxley after the conclusion of the seance explained to us that he had been promised a specimen of this particular plant to complete a collection and that the object of his visit to us had been to obtain it.

Another favorite feat of Yolande's was to put a glass of water into the hand of one of her particular friends and tell him to watch it. She would then hold her slender taper fingers over the glass and while his eyes were closely scrutinising the water within it a flower would form itself upon it and fill the glass. This upon inspection would generally be found to be a splendid specimen of some lovely rose with sometimes several blossoms on a stem.

Yolande's delight was equal to that of the favored friend when she succeeded in surprising him, but when we endeavored to learn how she did it she would shrug her shoulders and put her head on one side as though perplexed. I sometimes think she did not know herself how she produced these lovely flowers, but only acted under the supervision of her beloved Y-Ay-Ali who she said knew all about it. But Y-Ay-Ali, if she knew, kept the knowledge to herself, so far as we were concerned. Perhaps, if she had explained, we should have been no more able to produce

Ferns produced at a séance 12 April 1880.
The small piece to the left was handed as a pattern to
the spirit, and the two fronds to the right were
produced at the sitter's request.
(See following copy photo).

Ferns produced at a séance 12 April 1880.
After two ferns had been produced at the sitter's request,
the above were also handed to him by the spirit.
(See previous copy photo).

the same result as Yolande than we are now. But in any case the "modus operandi" of these lovely creations remains as much a mystery as ever to us.

Another of Yolande's pretty feats was to beg a water pitcher, and half filling it with water she would, by the help of one of the friends, lift it to her head or shoulder, carrying it there as she moved from one to another, forming a picture of oriental grace and beauty, with the dusky face and arms, the snowy garments, and the black waving hair falling over the pretty shoulders and swaying form. When, after saluting her friends, Yolande would lift the pitcher from her shoulder it would be found to be filled to the brim with dozens or scores of the most perfect roses, which she would generously distribute to the assembled company, generally offering them the pitcher and letting them help themselves. Sometimes flowers of a particular color would be asked for and always obtained.

Once someone remarked to me. "Why dont *you* ask for something?" I had really never thought of asking for anything myself, always being sufficiently interested in observing the actions of Yolande whenever I did by chance get an opportunity of seeing what was going on. But on hearing this query Yolande looked at me enquiringly and I asked her to give me a rose,—a black rose. That will puzzle her, I thought to myself, as I then hardly imagined such a flower existed. Instantly Yolande dipped her fingers into the pitcher and brought out a dark object, dripping with moisture, and handed it to me triumphantly. It was a rose of a distinctly blue black color, the like of which neither I nor any of those assembled had seen. It was a magnificent specimen, though valuable for its uniqueness rather than its beauty, at least to my taste.

This little attention on the part of Yolande was also worthy of remark, for she very seldom favored me with any notice, seeming rather to ignore me, or to accept my presence in the cabinet as a necessary evil.

There seemed to exist a strange link between us. I could do nothing to ensure her appearance amongst us. She came and went, so far as I am aware, entirely independent of my will, but when she had come, she was, I found, dependent on me for her brief material existence. I seemed to lose, not my individuality, but my strength and power of exertion, and though I did not then know it, a great portion of my material substance. I felt that in some way I was changed, but the effort to think logically in some mysterious way affected Yolande, and made her weak. The stronger and livelier she became the less inclination I had to think or reason, but the power of feeling became intensified to a painful extent; I do not mean in the physical sense, but the mental, my brain apparently becoming a sort of whispering gallery where the thoughts of other persons resolved themselves into an embodied form and resounded as though actual substantial objects. Was any one suffering, I felt the pain. Was any one worried or depressed, I felt it instantly. Joy or sorrow made themselves in some way perceptible to me. I could not tell *who* among the friends assembled was suffering, only that the pain existed and was in some way reproduced in myself.

If anyone left his or her seat, thus breaking the chain, this fact was communicated to me in a mysterious but unmistakable manner.

Sometimes Yolande's peregrinations caused me a vague anxiety. She evidently enjoyed her brief stay in our midst and was so bold, in spite of her apparent timidity, that I was often tormented by fears of what she might do and had a weird sort of feeling that any accident or imprudence on her part would fall back on myself, though in what way I had no clear idea. I had that to learn later.

If at any time my feeling of anxiety really took the shape of a thought, I discovered that it caused Yolande to return to the cabinet reluctantly always, and sometimes with a childish petulence, which showed that my thought exercised a compelling power over her actions, and that she only came back to me because she could not help herself.

Plants produced at a séance 8 March 1890.
(From a photograph).

Plants produced at a séance 8 March 1890.
(From a photograph).

The strawberry plant with fruit and flowers produced at a séance. The ripe fruit was partaken of by the sitters.

CHAPTER XX.

NUMEROUS SPIRIT VISITANTS.

"One of these men is genius to the other
And so of these, which is the natural man
And which the spirit? Who deciphers them?"

Comedy Of Errors, *scene I*

It must not be supposed that our spirit visitants were confined to Walter, Yolande, Ninia, and Y-Ay-Ali. Never a meeting passed but we were brought face to face with some strange visitor. Sometimes they passed again into the darkness of the unknown, and came to us no more. Others came, were recognized, and remained awhile with us—disappearing only to come again when next we met.

How many times have I thanked God for this wonderful gift which enabled me to bring such comfort to aching hearts! And bitterly as I have suffered from cruel persecutions at the hands of ignorant and unbelieving men, I thank God still.

One evening we were startled by the sudden appearance of a young sailor clad in his blue uniform, gold band and buttons, his cap with its peak and badge on his head. I saw him as the light fell on him when he parted the curtains and went out from the cabinet. His appearance surprised me because it was so like that of an ordinary person that I could not think it was a spirit. I had not had time to gather my thoughts, however, when I heard cries and exclamations of joy, which had the effect of breaking off the prayer our good Mr. H. was offering up. I saw nothing, I could only listen, but they told me afterwards that the scene which followed the sailor boy's entrance in the circle was very affecting. He had walked towards a lady seated farthest away from him, and she, recognizing her lost son, started forward, meeting him half way. He flung his arms around her in a passionate embrace, and they stood locked in each other's arms. Not many amongst us but shed tears of sympathy for the mother and son so strangely brought together!

"It is my son, my Alfred," said the lady; "my only child, whom I never thought to meet again. He is not altered, he is no taller, no stouter, no different in any way. The little moustache he was so proud of is just as it was when I bade him goodbye for the last time, when he left for the voyage from which he never returned. He is just my boy and no-one else. Nothing in the world can alter that great fact or take that comfort away from me, that my boy still lives and loves me as he always did."

Among the many sick persons who solicited the aid of our spirit friends was Mr. Hugh Biltcliffe of Gateshead, a personal friend of Mr. and Mrs. F. Unfortunately we heard of his illness too late to do more than render his last hours more free from pain, and to the grief of a large number of friends he passed on to the land ahead, a few days after the first intimation of his illness reached us. His widow and children were inconsolable. He had been a spiritualist but had never taken any active part in the propagation of his beliefs, although he was greatly interested in all educational movements, the temperance cause in particular being his special work. His wife, though sharing his views, had not interested herself much in the experiments in which we were engaged, and in fact after her husband's death I seldom saw her. I had not known either of them till just before his passing away, when he was greatly emaciated and altered in appearance, so that I never saw him in his ordinary aspect.

Mrs Biltcliffe some months after the death of her husband came to one of our evening meetings in company with Mr. and Mrs. F. and what followed I will give in the words of Mr. F. who afterwards published a statement signed by Mrs. Biltcliffe, and two other ladies who were also present at the time. He writes:—

"Mr. Hugh Biltcliffe, an esteemed friend of mine, died about twelve months ago. He was a man well known in Gateshead, took an active part in the temperance cause, and was for some years superintendent of a Sunday-school. Both he and his wife,

Mrs. Isabella Biltcliffe, were spiritualists, but she had never attended such a séance as I am about to discribe.

"When the séance was, as we thought, about to be closed there appeared at the opening of the curtains a fine tall well-built man with dark whiskers and dark hair, and clothed in long white robes. Altogether he had a majestic and noble appearance.

"In an instant I recognised in him my friend, Mr. Biltcliffe.

"What is most remarkable is the fact that not only did I recognise him, but his wife, my wife, and another lady present, all knew him immediately he appeared. Besides these there were two gentlemen, sitting further away, who mentioned my friend's name, and asked if they were correct in their surmise as to the identity of the form.

"Thus four persons recognised him without a doubt in their minds, whilst the other two, evidently knowing him, somewhat doubted the evidence of their senses.

"He came near me and reached forward to shake hands. His hand, which was somewhat larger than mine, was warm, soft, and natural. His grasp was firm and vigorous, as was his wont during his earthly life; and I accepted his fervent shake as an expression of thanks for little services I had rendered him during his illness.

"At a meeting ten days later Mrs. Biltcliffe came with her two little daughters, Agnes aged thirteen, and Sarah between seven and eight years af age.

"Again my friend came and showed himself to us, proving that, though we had laid him in the grave, he was still as much alive as we were and anxious to testify to the fact that there is no death.

"The moment he appeared before us his little daughter Sarah, a bright, intelligent child, ran to him, when he took her in his arms and kissed her. She clung to him as though she would never be parted from him again, and she had to be taken away by her elder sister who also embraced and kissed her father. Many, many questions they have asked such as:— 'Where did he get all the white clothes that he had?' 'What did he do with them when he went away?' 'How did he get into the room?' 'Did

I know him? Yes I knew him. Do you think I did not know my father?' 'How queer it is. He is dead you know, and he is alive. How is that?'

"These and a few hundred other queries and remarks puzzle wiser heads than theirs, but the wisest would not be able to persuade her that she had not positively seen and embraced her father who had been dead to her more than a year."

I will mention another instance of a similar nature, which interested me because I was personally acquainted with all the persons concerned. An elderly gentleman of my acquaintance had been a spiritualist for many years. His wife, who was not in the least in sympathy with his views of life, died about this time. I had not the same friendly feeling for her as for him, because when I had occasionally visited their home, her sharp speeches somewhat grated on me, and I felt sorry for the poor man, who I feared had to prosecute his studies under disadvantages to which I was a stranger.

However, she died, and it surprised me a little to find how much her loss affected my old friend. A few days after the funeral he came to the séance room, not with any intention of staying for the seance, but once there he stopped. I had felt very sorry for his grief and was glad he remained believing it would give him something else to think about than his present trouble. I do not remember exactly what took place at the beginning of the seance, but I distinctly recollect the curtains being thrown open with a jerk, letting the light fall full on the figure of Mrs. Miller. Used as I was by this time to all sorts of unbelievable things I fairly gasped with astonishment. There could be no mistake. Her every feature, her every gesture, was her own. She was instantly recognised by several who knew her. Her husband almost overcome with emotion would have embraced her but she turned from him asking sharply:—

"What have you done with my ring?"

A thunder clap could not have startled us more.

"My dear," replied the poor man, "I have not done anything with your ring; is it not on your finger?" And he fairly broke into sobs, and Mrs. M. went back into the cabinet from whence she had emerged. I positively felt as though I should have enjoyed shaking her.

Mr. M. seemed much distressed at her evident displeasure. He told us his wife had said before her death, that two rings, which she always wore, were not to be removed if she died, and he promised her that her wishes should be obeyed; further than this he knew nothing, nor did he understand her remark in the least. I fancy he did not feel the unkindness of her treatment either, but I am sure we most of us felt more or less indignation at the loving sorrowing heart being ignored and slighted for the sake of a ring, no matter how much it was valued.

Later, Mr. M. told us that on returning home he had questioned his daughter as to the rings, and had learned that she, not knowing of her mother's request, had removed them just prior to the funeral, thinking that her father would be pleased to have them afterwards. This, then, explained the sharp enquiry with which she met her husband. She came again several times and exchanged greetings with her friends, but I think she never conquered her prejudice to spiritualism, and only made use of our meetings when she had some object to attain. In spite of herself, however, the mere fact of her appearance was a sufficient testimony in favor of the subject she despised; for all who knew her, and they were not few, received convincing proofs that Mrs. M. at any rate was very much alive, and had not altered either in appearance or character.

In the study of these manifestations one's orthodox ideas of the inhabitants of the heavenly spheres receive some severe shocks. So far as I could judge, none of our spirit visitors answered to my preconceived idea of angelic beings, with the exception perhaps of Y-Ay-Ali. They seemed as human as ever they had been in life; and another occurrence in which a long conversation took place between a visitor to the rooms and a spirit, gave me food for thought for a very long while.

It was at the usual bi-weekly meeting. Two strangers, friends of one of the members, had been by general consent invited to take part in the séance, when a spirit appeared to me, a tall man, rather well made, with black hair, black moustache and beard,

and a forehead rather high and broad. As he was apparently unknown to us, we enquired whether there was anyone for whom
he came, and the figure gave us to understand that he knew one
of the strange gentlemen who was present. This gentleman at the
time objected to having his name made public, and I will therefore in recording the conversation designate him by the letter B.

Mr. B.: "Who is it? Is it Phillips?"
Spirit: "No."
Mr. B.: "Is it Lynch?"
Spirit: "Yes, Emmanuel Lynch."
Mr. B.: "I never thought about Emmanuel. It was Frank I
thought about; he died at sea."
Spirit: "No, I didn't die at sea; I died of consumption."
Mr. B.: "Yes that's right; I meant Frank died at sea, but Em-
manuel died at Hartlepool."
Spirit: "Yes at Old Hartlepool. Do you know whether my
father and mother are living? And is my wife alive? When do
you say Frank died? Is Ralph still living? What ship was I in
when you last saw me?"
Mr. B.: "I dont know which ship it was, but it was about
1867. I cannot answer positively your other questions as I have
not been at Hartlepool for some time."
Spirit: "I would like to see the old folks once more, or know
if they have left your world. The old man was bad enough before
I died, but then it was nothing fresh for him. To think he should
have been so strong and mother too, and all of us boys to die,—
nine of us of consumption."
Mr. B.: "I have heard there were nine boys, but Emmanuel
and Frank were the only ones I knew."
Spirit: "I wonder if Kate, my wife, is married again, but that
doesn't matter. Did you know Brough the ship's husband?"
Mr. B.: "No I didn't know the ship's husband."
Spirit: "Did you know old Captain Wynn?"
Mr. B.: "Yes, he is alive. I was talking to him today."
Spirit: "I dont mean that one. He lived in Poplar in London.
He died long before me. He is here now, and wants to send a

message to his wife. He wants to know if she is married again or has forgotten him, because if she has he won't bother her."

Mr. B.: "I do not know her address."

Spirit: "Write to John Fennick, 44 Coal Exchange, London, he will give you Mrs. Wynn's address. Ask Emily M. if she remembers Manny Lynch; she wanted to marry me."

Mr. B.: to the circle: "Manny Lynch, Yes we used to call him Manny. He got a sculptor to carve his bust when he was up in the Mediterranean."

Spirit: "Yes, Jack Rogers got his done too, and passed it off for Garibaldi."

Mr. B.: "Is Jack Rogers alive yet?"

Spirit: "He left me and went off in the 'Iron Age' and she was lost, but whether he was lost too I cannot say,"

Mr. B.: "I know the name of the ship 'Iron Age,' but I didn't know Jack Rogers, went in her. Have you seen Captain W—y lately?"

Spirit: "No I heard something about him just at the time I was took bad, but I don't remember what it was. Is he dead?"

Mr. B.: "Yes."

Spirit: "He was a real fine fellow. So is M.. Give my compliments to him and tell him I'd be glad of a yarn with him. Give my love to Emily—I am sorry I could not accommodate the two of them. Come here often, and we will have a chat about old times and fellows."

I never saw the stranger again, but wondered very much what his ideas of Heaven were after this conversation.

Emmanuel Lynch was, as far as I could judge, as much interested in the things which concerned his earthly life as ever he had been. His friend told us that Emmanuel, or Manny Lynch, had been an Engineer on board a steamer, and that there was not the shadow of a doubt but that the spirit was his very self and no other. They were both, the visitor and the spirit, entire strangers to me and indeed to most of our circle, and this conversation, which might have passed without remark among two friends meeting after years of separation, struck us as something eerie or uncanny. We had imbibed the idea that spirits did not need to ask such questions as did Emmanuel Lynch, but he seemed like one who had been on a long voyage and was eager to know what changes had taken place during his absence.

One evening while sitting quietly in the cabinet, listening to the remarks which were circulating outside, I heard some words spoken close to my ear, startling me into an upright position to listen more intently. I heard someone close to the cabinet speaking in French, and gathered that the words were addressed to a spirit form which was standing between the opening of the curtains. I had seen it go out towards the light, but the peculiar lassitude which I always felt while these forms were manifesting had prevented me from following the movements attentively, so that when I heard a strange language spoken to, and answered by, the spirit form, I awakened as it were to a sense of something new which was taking place, and the words "Ma Petite, Ma Fille" excited so wild a curiosity within me that I felt I must see the speaker.

I obtained permission to leave my seat in the cabinet and on going feebly and with difficulty outside the curtains to where the white-robed figure stood, I came face to face with— myself!— or so it seemed to me.

The figure was a little taller, a little broader, the hair longer, the features, particularly the eyes, larger; but looking into the face, I might have been regarding my own reflexion in a mirror, so great was the resemblance.

She put her hands on my shoulders, and regarding me attentively murmured "Mignonne, Ma Petite."

Glad as I was at seeing face to face a dear but hitherto unknown relative, the sensation of amazed bewilderment prevailed over every other. I could not say that I recognised her, for my eyes had never knowingly rested on her before; still of her identity I had no doubt, though the strange resemblance to myself was a revelation. I had never heard that I bore any likeness to her, and I knew no one living who had known her, and of whom I might enquire.

She, whom we got afterwards to know by the title of "the French Lady," was one of our very few visitors from the spirit world, who seemed able to converse with us by speech, the greater number making themselves understood by signs or gestures in answer to questions put to them. Although she was, as we all knew, my particular friend, and came to us chiefly for my sake, she paid less attention to me than to the other members of our circle. Perhaps the peculiar part I had to take in the seances prevented her from shewing her affection, as she found that anything specially occupying my mind or arousing my interest caused a decrease in her power while in our midst. However it was, she paid a good deal more attention to others in the circle, particularly to Mr. F., who happened to be the only one there who could converse with her in her native language. She became a frequent visitor, seeming to find a pleasure in our society. Curiously enough she rapidly took note of one or two of our circle who were of the Roman Catholic religion, and became as it were more at ease with them than with the others. On one occasion one of these Catholic ladies presented our "French Lady" with a rosary with a small medal attached, which she said, if I remember rightly, had been blessed by the pope. The "French Lady" took the beads, and quickly detaching the medal walked across the room to the fireplace, where a fire was burning and deliberately dropped the medal into it, to the horror of the lady who had presented it. On being questioned as to her reason for so doing, she replied coolly that it required purifying.

When the medal was afterwards found in the ashes it was bright and clean! The next time she came, it was offered to her and after inspecting it closely, she permitted it to be attached again to the rosary, which was kept for her use and of which she seemed fond.

For quite a long while she was a never failing visitor to our séances, her great resemblance to myself being always a source of wonder and comment. Separately, we were frequently mistaken the one for the other. When standing together, the small differences I have spoken of were apparent and noticeable. On one occasion, however, a clergyman of the church of England was present. We, the "French Lady" and I, were side by side when she held out her hand to him to shake hands. He glanced first at the one of us, and then at the other, finally became bewildered and nervous, when he saw the two so much alike, that he did not know which was the spirit and which was I. Instead of taking her proffered hand, he grasped that of his next neighbour and thrust it forward!

CHAPTER XXI.

A BITTER EXPERIENCE.

"Experience is a hard schoolmaster."
CARLYLE

I HAVE hesitated a little whether or not to record the story of the bitter experience which I and our circle went through, and which had for its result long years of suffering both mental and physical, to me in particular. But as this is a faithful record of part of my work and experience, I feel that I ought not to withhold it. The most valuable lessons in life are often those which have cost us most suffering, and though I strongly resented the undeserved pain I endured at the time, the lesson I learned has opened my understanding of the mysteries of spirit phenomena, better than a life time of success could have done. In fact the success which attended our experiments had to a great extent blinded me, and perhaps all of us, to the delicate nature of the conditions required to produce the manifestations. Unconsciously to ourselves, or perhaps intuitively, not knowing why, we had adopted many of the means necessary to success, and the result seemed to warrant the idea, that we had only to set our energies to work in order to obtain anything we wanted in the way of phenomena.

How these things were produced was a matter we did not profess to understand. We knew that the presence of some persons was favorable, and that of others was not, and that extremes of weather were not good. A thunderstorm was inimical and a certain preventative of good results, but beyond these most elementary rules I do not think we had gained any positive knowledge. We were feeling our way blindly and, the success we had was apparently more owing to a series of lucky accidents, than to a scientific knowledge of what was required to bring it about.

Our very success was a source of danger to us. I have already spoken of the vague sense of uneasiness which Yolande's actions caused me. Although regarding her as a perfectly free and independent agent, accountable to no earthly authority, I could never divest myself of a sort of anxiousness about her, something akin to what a mother feels when her child is getting beyond her control and she fears it may overstep the line which she conceives should mark the boundary of the proprieties. I dont think my anxiety ever expressed itself in words; in fact, I did not know of what I was afraid.

My friend Mrs. F. was about to leave England, and I had decided to accompany her. The series of seances—not the first series by many—was drawing to a close, and I timed my departure by their completion. The strain of work was beginning to tell on me, and I was looking forward to a long rest with no small degree of pleasure. We had been engaged in packing our belongings, household furniture, pictures, china &c, and were feeling tired out with the unusual work, when, after seeing the last waggon-load safely on board the vessel that was to carry them to our northern home, we went to the house of the friend with whom we were to stay during the few days which must elapse before we left England.

I would have given much to retire early to bed instead of sitting in a séance, but as they were all expecting me, I had no alternative but to take my usual place amongst my friends promising myself a rest and doze in the cabinet.

The unusual work and worry attendant on the completion of all odds and ends, paintings, a bazaar for which I had promised sundry sketches, paying and receiving visits, my sick patients whom I was loath to leave, in addition to the actual removal of our household had caused me several sleepless nights, and anxious busy days, so that I was not feeling the slightest interest in what the spirits were doing, beyond the hope that they would not keep me there very long that evening, and thinking that when I did get to bed, I would stay there till noon next day. I do not know how long the séance had proceeded, but I knew that Yolande had taken her pitcher on her shoulder and was outside the cabinet. What actually occurred I had to learn afterwards. All I knew was I a horrible excruciating sensation of being doubled up and squeezed together, as I can imagine a hollow gutta percha doll would feel, if it had sensation, when violently embraced by its baby owner. A sense of terror and agonizing pain came over me, as though I were losing hold of life and was falling into some fearful abyss, yet knowing nothing, seeing nothing, hearing nothing, except the echo of a scream which I heard as at a distance. I felt I was sinking down, I knew not where. I tried to save myself, to grasp at something, but missed it; and then came a blank from which I awakened with a shuddering horror and sense of being bruised to death.

My senses seemed to have been scattered to the winds, and only little by little could I gather them sufficiently together to understand in a slight degree what had happened. Yolande had been seized and the man who had seized her declared it was I.

This was what I was told. The statement was so extraordinary, that if it had not been for my utter prostration I could have laughed, but I was unable to think or even move. I felt as though very little life remained in me, and that little was a torment. The hemorrhage of the lungs, which my residence in the south of Europe had apparently cured, broke out again and the blood almost I suffocated me. A severe prolonged illness was the result; and our departure from England was delayed for some weeks as I could not be moved.

The shock was a terrible one, and what was worse to me, than the shock itself, was my utter inability to understand it. It never occurred to me that any one would dare accuse me of imposition. I had, in my own estimation at least, been a Cæsar's wife. I had worked, together with my friends, at first from an inherent desire for knowledge, and later from pure love of the cause itself and a desire to propagate it.

The action of the man himself, who had seized Yolande, gave me less concern than did the revengeful spirit which actuated another sometime member of our circle. He was an artist of no mean order, and his hints and suggestions relative to my paintings were of value to me. I wished to repay his instructions in current coin of the realm, but this he would not accept, suggesting that between such kindred spirits money was a question that might not be discussed. He was imbued with some, to me, repulsive ideas on affinityship, which caused me to shun his society, and this was I believe the reason for the change of front which he showed towards me, and the false reports which he circulated.

He is gone to the next world now, and may see that in injuring one's neighbour one is lessening one's own chances of happiness. I never saw him again and was sorry when shortly afterwards I heard of his death in a lunatic asylum, where I learned he had previously been, at intervals, confined. I had not known of this, but it explained many of the peculiar and extraordinary ideas which he had been fond of promulgating, and which I had been at a loss to understand.

I did not blame the man so much who was the first cause of the trouble. He probably thought nothing of the sacrifices I was making, nothing of the work we had done, nothing of the years of study which had led up to our present position. He was an Iconoclast and thought he did well in destroying the false gods, as he considered them. I have thought that he was to be excused for his suspicion when I have remembered the extraordinary likeness between myself and the "French Lady" whom he had frequently seen; and then Yolande's proximity and naïve natural-ness, her utter "humanness" if I may use the word, were too much for him, in his ignorance.

CHAPTER XXII.

A FRESH BEGINNING.

"God forbid that I should do this thing and flee away from them…let us die manfully…let us not stain our honor."

MACCABEES I. CH. 9. V. 10.

THE result of this calamity was, in the first instance, an entire break-down in my health; in the second, a perfect horror of the name of spiritualistic phenomena, which, in deference to my wishes, were a tabooed subject of conversation for some years. However, in the clear air and sunshine of Sweden and the outdoor-life I led, roaming in the forests, sailing on the lakes, at work in my garden, riding or driving, it was not long before my health improved, though it did not become entirely re-instated for several years.

With returning strength I was, able in a great measure to throw off the depression which hung over me, and I found myself, in spite of my resolution to the contrary, wondering over the why and the wherefore of the disaster. However, situated as I was for a long time in the midst of a simple primitive God-fearing people, whose faith in God and the teachings of their Bible, had never been shaken, there was happily no need for the exercise of my powers, except as a means of helping the sick. Then indeed the power of the spirit would make itself known and valued. In this region of almost primeval forests, where the cottagers live on little patches of arable land in the midst of woods, widely separated from neighbours or from intercourse with the outer world, the people live hard poor lives, growing the rye to make their bread and a few potatoes which must be cared for like living things, to preserve them from the bitter frosts of the long winter. These things, the rye and potatoes, form their staple articles of food and they are lucky indeed if their patch of ground will produce enough to enable them to sell or exchange a part for the cotton or wool to weave into clothing for the family, which is the winter occupation, when the earth is hard frozen. Poor, very' poor, are they, but content withal as long as they have health and strength, but when accident or sickness comes then indeed is their fate sorrowful.

We had many people to think and care for and a doctor who had to attend them when sick, but he seemed to set very little value on the lives of his patients, or at least on the lives of his *poor* patients; and if he was sent for during a bad mid-winter day he displayed considerable reluctance in setting out on a long cold journey by sledge. And if after eliciting all the information possible with respect to the patient, he considered the case was not one of life or death, or was one where the patient was not of sufficient importance from a social point of view to cause him trouble in consequence of being neglected, he invariably decided to postpone his visit till a finer day. I do not think many doctors are like the gentleman to whom I allude, but so he was; consequently the poor people for many miles around came to us for help in sickness, as it was known that we kept a supply of the simpler remedies on hand, which precaution was necessary, as we lived several miles from the nearest town.

My clientèle rapidly increased and the good offices of my spirit friends were constantly in request. The doctor after awhile, invariably supplied the medicines they suggested. Not that he believed in spirits, but as long as I did not want poisons he cheerfully accepted my diagnoses and wrote the prescriptions I wanted, well pleased to be saved a tiresome journey.

Strange to say only two deaths occurred on the estates during our residence there and they were of persons who had been entirely under the doctors charge.

This was the only way in which I exercised my mediumistic gifts for a long time, till the ever recurring changes of life again brought me in contact with persons who were making a study of spiritualism and its phenomena. These were mostly such students of the philosophy of spiritualism as had not themselves made any practical experiments. Some of these were the friends who had previously helped me with their sympathy, and I could not but have a warm feeling of gratitude towards those who, in spite of slanderous reports, held out a hand of friendship and assured me of their undiminished faith.

A series of séances was arranged, having for their object the photographing of the materialised forms, and in this we were successful. A full report of our experiments was published in the "Medium and Daybreak" for March 28, 1890 and the photographs we obtained were reproduced in the same magazine for the 18th of April of the same year. These photographs were taken by the aid of magnesium light, and although I was much interested in the success of the experiments the light acted very injuriously on my nerves, which during a seance are sensitive to a high degree.

It was during these experiments that I began to attribute some peculiar after-effects of seances to their rightful cause. From the very beginning of our experiments in this line I had always more or less suffered from I nausea and vomiting after a séance for materialisation, I had grown to accept this as a natural consequence and not to be avoided. This had always been the case, except when surrounded only by the members of our home circle or children. During the course of seances for photography this unpleasantness increased so much that I was usually prostrate for a day, or sometimes two, after a sitting, and, as the symptoms were those of nicotine poisoning, experiments were made and it was discovered that none of these uncomfortable sensations were felt when seances were held with non-smokers. Again, when sick persons were in the circle, I invariably found myself feeling more or less unwell afterwards. With persons accustomed to the use of alcohol the discomfort was almost as marked as with smokers.

These séances were to me fruitful in many respects. I learned that many habits, which are common to the generality of mankind and sanctioned by custom, are deleterious to the results of a séance, or, at any rate to the health of the medium. Possibly I had become more sensitive to these influences, as I had not noticed the ill effects so strongly when in England, or it is possible that

Yolande as she appeared when materialised.
Photographed by magnesium light 8 March 1890.

it was due to one of the lucky accidents that very few of our English circle were smokers. I do not know how it was, but all or nearly all of the Swedish circle were smokers, and I had to suffer for it.

Another result of these séances was one so entirely unlooked for that for weeks afterwards I frequently caught myself wondering if it were not all a bad dream from which I should soon awake.

The seances had not been at first arranged with any intention of carrying them on regularly. They originated as follows:—

"One of my boy friends said to me Auntie! Tomorrow is my birthday. Are you going to give me a present?"

"Perhaps. Why?"

"Because if you are and you have not got it already, I would like a séance instead. You see I've told a lot of people about them and they're always at me to get them invited to a séance, so I thought if you would not mind I would like that better than a present."

I consented pleased that he should take so much interest in the subject; Ernest however found the difficulties in arranging a circle greater than he had anticipated and some days elapsed before all was in order. He was overwhelmed with applications for permission to attend, but the numbers had not to exceed twenty to twenty five. All invited were comparative strangers to me personally, although I knew most of them by name.

One among them the son of the editor of a local newspaper, was I learned afterwards an enthusiastic theosophist, and professed the greatest possible interest in the result of the séance,— he was also a photographer and it was owing to this fact that I agreed to the proposal of photographing the materialised forms.

The idea once mooted was encouraged and a series of séances for the purpose of photographic experiments was arranged, most of the assistants at the birthday seance agreeing to take part in them.

A faithful and minute record of each séance was kept by the photographer above named who pursued the investigation with

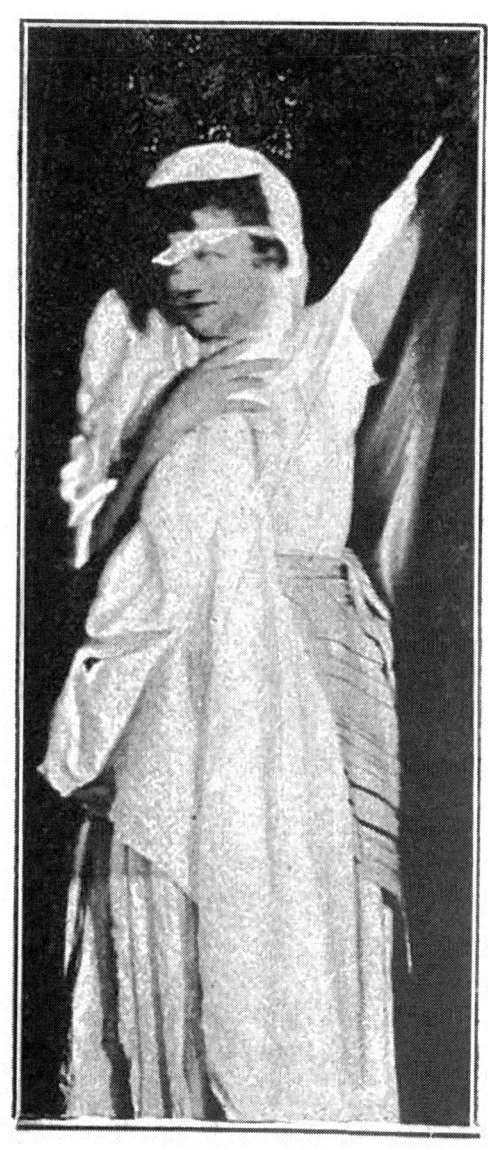

Leila as materialised 13 March 1890.
(Photographed by magnesium light).

the liveliest interest, his enthusiasm infecting the others, the results were far beyond what we had anticipated.

The manifestations appeared to receive no check in consequence of the severe tests which were tried, indeed it seemed to me that our unseen friends were put on their mettle to triumph over all obstacles placed in their way which they did with perfect success.

Several photographs were taken by aid of the magnesium light, copies of which are reproduced here namely the portraits of "Yolande" and "Leila." These photographs which were to us a source of satisfaction and congratulation became in the hands of our enemies an excuse for an attack upon me personally. Whether the photographer simulated the enthusiastic interest he shewed, or whether he was himself a victim to his friends rapacity for "copy" I do not know. I prefer to think he was made a tool of by his friends, and thus give him the benefit of the doubt. As before mentioned he kept careful notes of each séance, and at the end of them he brought me a manuscript which he proposed with my consent to publish at some future time, because the conditions of admission had been that the experiments were to be considered strictly private and nothing was to be published unless I wished it. The photographer as well as the others agreed to this. I read his manuscript hastily through, made a copy, struck out my name wherever its was written in full, and returned the original to him, pleased with the impartial manner in which he had dealt with the subject, and the keen observation which he had displayed throughout the entire series. In this manuscript he expressed himself as having certain convictions as well as certain doubts, but to these I had no objection, his views and opinions being in many respects the same as my own. A man who has no doubts to overcome in this investigation is not likely to prove a powerful ally.

When however the article appeared a few days later without my consent or the consent of the other sitters it was in such a mutilated condition interspersed by aspersions and accusations that I felt half paralysed with horror, scarcely believing my senses.

Leila as she appeared materialised 13 March 1890.
(Photographed by magnesium light).

I could not understand how anyone could profess so much friendship, take so much pains to write impartially, and at the same time publish views which were diametrically opposite to the facts related, not only by himself but by the other sitters.

When I place the two articles alongside of each other, and try to explain them, it seems to me impossible that one and the same person can have written them.

Space does not allow me to produce both articles here, but in a future volume I intend to give them verbatim and leave my readers to unravel the mystery of the truth and its distorted but apparent reflection.

I have no personal motive to serve nor desire to injure a mis-guided opponent whose name I do not even mention. As this work however may fall into the hands of some who only read the mutilated reports and may consider that my silence gave color to the falsehoods and thereby to some extent stamped them as truths—seeing that up to the present time I have not published his report of the séances, which would have clearly shown that the public had been duped—it is simply from a sense of duty to the public, and to those in particular who have been misled by the false reports that I am induced to give this explanation.

The reports referred to were copied into every newspaper in the country, enlarged upon, added to, or altered, leading articles of the most vicious character appeared in several more or less prominent newspapers entertaining the people of Sweden for a space of three weeks. During this time the indignation of my personal friends who gathered about me, was so great that, I had to interfere to prevent some schemes for chastising the offenders being carried into effect.

Except for the loyal partisanship of some of my friends I could not have borne the misery of this time. Every one advised me to go away for awhile, even he—the originator of the scandal probably unnerved by the storm he had raised was the first to advise this. Although I would have liked to have left it all—to have escaped from the anonymous letter writers who regaled me daily with the base outpourings of their own dishonorable natures,—to have fled from the insults which met me at every turn, I was afraid, afraid lest by turning my back on the enemy, color would be given to their accusations. So I stayed at my post and tried to attend to my daily work.

It was a terrible ordeal, and had it not been for the consciousness that I had done nothing to merit it, I must have broken down. As it was, my health began to suffer severely from the constant strain, and it was sometimes with difficulty I could summon courage enough to take my usual daily walks and to hear myself pointed out in significant tones by the passers by.

It was at this juncture that the motto taught me when a little child by my father "*Fais ce que tu dois, advienne qui pourra*" became a sort of sheet anchor. I found myself often repeating the words and finding support and courage in them.

So I remained, and the tide turned, for a reaction set in. The violence of the penny-a-liners awakened an antagonistic element even among persons who had previously not given the subject of spiritualism a moments consideration; a spirit of chivalry was aroused, to defend a woman who was being mercilessly persecuted. Friends gathered about me then and the cause for which I had labored gained many earnest supporters, who might perhaps never have heard of the subject except for the unmerited blame under which I lay.

Later in the same year another series was held, this time for an old and valued friend the Hon. A. Aksakof of St. Petersburg, who together with some Russian friends came on a visit to our home. Photographing the materialised forms being the object worked for, the circle was composed in this case only of the members of our household, and our Russian friends, with one or two whom we considered the most suitable, chosen from amongst those who had assisted at the earlier series.

Many photographs were taken but none were thoroughly successful; at least not in the way we wanted, though we obtained many things we did not expect or try for. Some of these unexpected results were very interesting, one of them being the accidental photographing of a man's face while focussing the cabinet and trying the magnesium light, in order to know how to do it without a hitch on the following day when the seance was to be held.

When the light was flashed, there was a general exclamation "I saw a man's face behind Mrs. E." Consequently the plate was developed, and sure enough there was a man's face as distinct as my own, to be seen above and behind my chair; a face considerably better to look at than my own, for the brightness of the flashlight had caused me to screw up my eyes and features till they presented an extraordinary spectacle. Who the man was, Walter afterwards explained to us.

The story in full was published in the "Medium and Daybreak" for 21 April 1893, and afterwards published in book-form in Scandinavia and Germany, under the title "The dead are living." The story of the incident as recorded is too long to reproduce here, but the principal facts are as follow:

One day the 3rd April 1890, I was busily engaged writing business letters, when, hesitating for some words, my hand wrote the name "Sven Strömberg." Vexed at having spoiled my letter, I tossed the paper into a drawer and forgot it, but happened to mention the incident in a letter which was copied later in the day.

On enquiring of Walter if he knew who the man was, who had been photographed, he replied in writing: "Oh yes, he is called 'Sven Strömberg:' died in America or Canada the 31st or 13th of March, I forget which; says he used to live in a place called Jemland, or something like that; but anyway he is dead, and his wife and half a dozen children are in America. He wants you to tell his people that he is dead,—died greatly respected and lamented, and all that."

In reply to this we asked for fuller information, but Walter seemed to have forgotten the details. The next day he wrote us that Sven Strömberg had emigrated with his young wife from his native village of Ström, the name of which he had adopted on his arrival in Canada. He settled in an out-of-the-way corner, called New Stockholm, where children were born to him, and where he died on 31st March 1890, three days before he wrote his name with my hand on a half finished letter. He had asked his wife to communicate the news of his illness and death to his parents and relatives in the old country, and as she had not done so he was anxious they should be informed; hence his recent appearance among us.

The whole story was told in Walter's peculiar humerous manner, interspersed with remarks respecting the late Sven Strömberg's anxiety to let his friends in Sweden understand that he had become of some importance in his Canadian settlement.

Mr. F. undertook to inform the people in Ström of Sven's death. The story was related to Consul Öhlén, the Swedish representative in Winnepeg, and he was asked to make enquiries as to the truth thereof. Being much struck with it, he published Mr. Ps letter in the "Canadensaren" and the "Manitoba Free Press," and the result was that eveny confirmation was obtained of the actual truth of every particular narrated by Walter, and further, that some one having read the newspaper report, carried it to Mrs. S. Strömberg, the widow, who confessed that, though she had written to her relatives in Ström in Sweden, the nearest post office being a journey of twelve miles, she had not had time to take her letter there, her husband's death having left so much on her hands. She became so frightened on reading the letter of Mr. F. in the newspaper, that the poor woman set off immediately to post her letter.

Such in short are the particulars of the case. The whole of the voluminous correspondence, which the elicitation of these facts entailed, together with the verification of all the statements, is in the possession of Mr. Fidlr, of Gothenburg, who went to an immense amount of trouble in investigating this matter.

Another unexpected manifestation was one which interested me more than "Sven Strömberg," whose name I grew to dislike, so often did I hear it repeated. This was Yolande's greatest production and indeed her last,—for after it she bade us farewell and left us, as we then thought, not to return.

CHAPTER XXIII.

THE GOLDEN LILY—YOLADE'S LAST WORK.

"Take of everyone of them a rod,…write thou every man's name upon his rod…And it came to pass that on the morrow, Moses went into the tabernacle of witness; and, behold, the rod of Aaron, for the house of Levi, was budded, and brought forth buds, and bloomed blossoms and yielded almonds."

NUMBERS, CH. 17, V. 2 AND 8

THIS last work of Yolande's was one of the unexpected incidents which occurred during what we grew to call the Aksakof séances. Although rich in unlooked-for results, we had been unable to obtain the particular object for which these séances were being held, and I was beginning to fear that our efforts would be fruitless. This continued strain, and other worries of a business character, were beginning to tell on my nerves, and the knowledge that this in itself was inimical to success was an unquieting thought. At the same time it is most difficult to throw off anxiety at command, and though I did my best, it was not much to be proud of. On the evening of the 28th June 1890, we assembled in our usual séance room. It was in reality the upper Hall of the house, an octagon shaped chamber, lighted from the roof by a large ornamental glass window, which we had. so arranged that a softly tinted mild light was admitted equally to all parts of the room. The conditions in every respect seemed as bad as they could possibly be. In the first place I had accidently scorched my arm. In lighting a hanging lamp, a piece of the match had fallen on my dress and the thin muslin was instantly in a blaze. My arms were bare and though the flame was quickly extinguished my left arm was painfully scorched. In addition to this I had been suffering from a slight but irritating toothache all day.

These little discomforts, together with a violent storm of wind which shook the house to its foundations, did not promise much for the success of our seance. We proposed postponing it till next day, but found it was not convenient for most of our friends, all having other engagements; and on referring the matter to Walter, he told us that Yolande particurlarly desired us to try that evening.

After this we had no alternative but to take our places at once. For every one to get quietly composed was not an easy matter; the sound of doors and windows in other parts of the house being forced in by the wind, and sundry breaking of glass panes, had a most disquieting and irritating effect on everybody's nerves and on mine in particular. The storm decreased in violence as the evening wore away, but judging from experience it seemed to me a hopeless attempt to continue sitting under such conditions, and I was about to propose giving it up, when I noticed a scent of flowers, which increased so much as to be almost overpowering. I am not fond of strong perfumes, and this nearly made me sick with its sweetness.

Walter gave us a message requesting us to keep as quiet and composed as we could and that no one was to talk to me, because Yolande was about to bring us a flower; and the external conditions being so bad we must do all we could to help her.

We did what we could, and the fact that we had something to expect helped to put us in a better humour. We had sand, water, and a flowerpot in readiness, as we were accustomed, though they had never been asked for during many months.

The strong scent was so overpowering, that I felt half suffocated. I put out my hand expecting to feel flowers, but there was nothing. Immediately afterwards, something large, heavy, cold, and damp fell against me. My first thought was that it was some dead clammy body or object, and it gave me such a horrid sensation that I almost fainted. I was holding the hand of Mr. Aksakof, when it began to feel as though I was receiving a succession of electric shocks, making it painful for me to come in contact with anything, each shock causing the perspiration to rush from every pore in my skin.

The pain from my scorched arm left me, and the toothache also was forgotten; and strangely enough every one noticed that Yolande carried her arm as though she were in pain, and when accidently touched she flinched as though hurt. I felt very thirsty and drank much water, but that was nothing unusual during a seance. What went on outside the curtains I learned afterwards from Mr. F's notes. Yolande with the assistance of Mr. Aksakof had mixed sand and loam in the flower pot and she had covered it with her veil, as she had done in the case of the water bottle in England when the Ixora Crocata was grown.

The white drapery was seen to rise slowly but steadily, widening out as it grew higher and higher. Yolande stood by and manipulated the gossamer-like covering till it reached a height far above her head, when she carefully removed it, disclosing a tall plant bowed with a mass of heavy blossom, which emitted the strong sweet scent I had complained of.

Notes were taken of its size, and it was found to be about seven feet in length from root to point, or about a foot and half taller than myself. Even when bent by the weight of the eleven large blossoms it bore, it was taller than I. The flowers were very perfect, measuring eight inches in diameter; five were fully blown, three were just opening, and three in bud, all without spot or blemish, and damp with dew. It was most lovely, but somehow the scent of lilies since that evening has always made me feel faint.

Yolande seemed very pleased with her success and told us that if we wanted to photograph the Lily we were to do so, as she must take it away again. She stood beside it and Mr. Boutlerof photographed it and her, twice. Mr. B. said "They are not very beautiful specimens of the photographic art," but there they were, and taking into consideration the woeful conditions the only thing to wonder at is that they could be obtained at all. The photographing was done by aid of the magnesium flash light. When this had been concluded, we were told to remain perfectly quiescent to enable Yolande to dematerialise the plant. We tried to comply with the request, but under the circumstances it was scarcely possible to feel indifferent enough to what was going on

The Golden Lily, produced at a séance, 28 June 1890.
Was kept a week, during which time six photographs
were taken, after which it dissolved and disappeared.

to be perfectly quiet. The consequence was that after sitting till midnight Yolande despairingly told us that she could not take the plant away.

Walter wrote:—"Yolande only got the plant on condition she brought it back. She finds the medium is exhausted and cannot bear any more. You must let the plant remain in darkness till she can come again and take it."

Mr. Fidler and Mr. Boutlerof then between them carried the plant to a dark closet in an adjoining room, where it was locked up, till we should receive instructions how to act with respect to it. We had been told that no light must be allowed to fall on it as that would increase Yolande's difficulty in removing it, but curiosity got the better of us and we brought the plant into the drawing-room one morning and photographed it four times in various positions, so that although we were not to keep the strangely grown plant itself, we have the best of evidence that it had existed in absolute incontrovertible reality.

I felt very sorry for Yolande; she seemed distressed for the fate of the great Lily which was visibly beginning to suffer. I think she had made three attempts to take it before she succeeded, and the last was on the 5th of July—eight days after the plant had grown up in our midst, when it vanished as mysteriously as it had come. All we knew was that at 9.23 p.m. the plant stood in our midst, and at 9.30 it was gone; not a vestige remained to show that it had ever existed, except the photographs we had taken and a couple of flowers which had fallen off. The soil was emptied out of the pot where it had stood for eight days, but no sign of it was left. Several of our circle declared that the plant vanished instantly. The scent seemed for a moment to fill the room almost overpoweringly, and then was gone; the exact moment of its disappearance could not be agreed upon nor the manner of its going, but gone it was.

During the week the Lily was in our possession we had several conversations with Walter with respect to it. We wanted permission before taking upon ourselves the responsibility of photographing it and asked Walter to help us to obtain it. We first asked:—"What has to be done with the Lilium Auratum?"

The Golden Lily and medium. The plant when straight
measured 7 ft; when bent as seen above its
height was about 6 ft.

"Well, that is more than I know. Yolande is anxious about it and wants to try again to-night to take it."

"Can we not pay for it and keep it?"

"You might if you knew where it came from, but she cannot tell that herself. Any way it has got to go if she can manage it; if she cannot then it must stop."

"In what does the absolute necessity of taking it back consist?"

"Have you not learned so much of your catechism? She has been told not to take things which did not belong to her. It's no use reasoning with one of her sex, she says it's got to go and I suppose it will have to."

"May we take it out and look at it and check some of its measurements?"

"I don't know. Yolande gave orders it might not be in the light."

"We have watered it."

"Don't do anything else or she will blame me."

"Please give us an explanation of how the plant was brought."

"I cannot, I only know it was here before you were last night, and was ready for being put together at least an hour before you saw it."

"Do you mean it was here before we came to the séance?"

"Before any one came to the séance. Yolande told me she had it ready and was afraid the bad conditions would prevent her materialising it."

Another curious little circumstance with respect to the Lily was that Yolande, not being able to tell us where she got the plant, said she would let us know in another way. On the night of its disappearance, before it vanished, a piece of grey cloth was found to be on the stem of it; the stem was in fact through a hole in the centre of the cloth. How it came there was a mystery like all the rest. It was not there when we photographed the plant in daylight. Yet to all appearance it had grown there, and could not be removed. Yolande, however instructed Mr. Aksakof to draw it from the stem, which he did; there was no rent in it, nothing but the round hole through which the stem had passed. She told us that she got the piece of cloth from the same country as the flower had grown. On examination the piece of grey cloth was found to be a scrap of mummy cloth, still aromatic with the perfumes used in embalming.

This led us to infer that the plant had been brought from Egypt. Sometime previously Mr. Oxley had given Mr. F. a piece of mummy cloth from one of the royal tombs in the pyramids. It was considered to be of very fine texture compared with cloths used for embalming less important personages. It contained 1008 meshes to the square inch whereas that on the Lily contained 2584 meshes to the square inch.

CHAPTER XXIV.

SHALL I BE "ANNA" OR "ANNA" BE I?

For some time after these experiments my powers sank to a very low ebb and after trying once or twice in vain to obtain some writing or simple manifestations, I gave it up and devoted all my attention to my daily work, and to painting, which I took up with increased pleasure as some of my productions had been rewarded with a first prize at an art competition, and one or two of my Swedish landscapes were sold at prices which gave me great hope for the future.

I went in for hard study for a year intending to make a long holiday in Norway in the following summer for the purpose of sketching. The sale of a picture or two made me the proud possessor of funds enough for a lengthy tour, and I set off with the determination to enjoy myself without stint.

I am very fond of this "Land of the midnight sun" with its fjelds and fjords and its wild rugged scenes; its glorious skies, its remnants of the worship of the old gods, its weird stories and superstitions; the land of Odin, of Thor and the Valkyria who watched for the souls of the warriors who fell in battle, to bear them away to Valhalla. I love its people, the hardy Scandinavian, with their free independence of thought, their honest straightforward simplicity of speech and chivalrous defence of what they deem to be right. Honest themselves they expect others to be the same, not only honest in deed but in thought. They will not shirk a duty because it is unpleasant or because their motives may be misunderstood, and what they undertake they go through with energy, whether it is enquiry into spiritualism or a voyage to the North Pole.

It was to assist some of these good friends that I was induced to take up the experiments of materialisation again, this time in a more studious and critical spirit than before. I felt that in spite of my experience of these phenomena, I was as far from under-standing them as were those who had yet to begin their study. I had read much of séances with other mediums, and had prided myself on the fact that under all circumstances I had retained my senses and had not been entranced and unconscious as they were. Still I could not see that my senses had been of much use to me in enabling me to understand the *modus operandi* of the manifestations. With these people I felt that I should in some way be helped. They in the first place appeared to know more of the theory and philosophy than I did. They noticed and com-mented on things which had either escaped my observation or had not been considered of importance. Thus I began as it were a fresh study.

From the beginning I decided that, whether we obtained any manifestations or not, I would not sit behind curtains again. I would use my eyes as well as my ears. If a cabinet was absolutely necessary as we had been so I often told it was, well,—then we would have a cabinet, but I would sit outside of it.

This resolve made it rather uphill work, and at first it seemed useless to proceed, as the necessity for darkness made it almost impossible to see the forms when they did appear. But this grew better as we went on, and at last I began to think I was on the right road to learn. I could observe what went on and was not dependent on my ears alone for information. In spite of this I was no nearer really finding out how these things happened. I saw they did happen, I saw the results, but the how and the *why* remained an impenetrable mystery.

It was at one of these séances in Christiania that a sitter "ab-stracted" a piece of the drapery which clothed one of the spirit forms. Later I discovered that a large square piece of material was missing from my skirt, partly cut, partly torn out. My dress was of a heavy dark woollen material. The "abstracted" piece of drapery was found to be of the same shape as that missing from my skirt; but several times larger, and white in color, the texture fine and thin as gossamer!

Something of the kind had happened once before in Eng-land, when some one had begged the little Ninia for a piece of her abundant clothing. She complied, unwillingly it seemed and the reason for her unwillingness was explained when, after the séance, I found a hole in a new dress which I had put on for the first time. This being nearly black I had attributed the mishap more to an accident on the part of Ninia than to any psychological cause. Now that it happened a second time, I began to understand that it was no accident, and that my dress, or the clothing of the persons in the séance, was the foundation of or the stores from which the dazzling raiment of the spirit form was drawn. The same thing has occurred once or twice since, but when the spirit has given willingly, or has itself cut the piece off its garment, my dress has escaped mutilation.

The experiments made with my good friends under these new conditions were of intense interest to me and gave me much food for thought. I had begun to have a feeling of dissatisfaction with respect to these materialised forms. I could not analyse my own feelings with respect to them, but a vague sense of doubt that had not yet grown into a thought, began to puzzle me. I hardly knew how it arose or where it came from, but I could not get away from it,—it haunted me constantly.

Now that I became, as it were, one of the circle instead of occupying the isolated position within the cabinet as I had previously done, I had a point of double observation, inasmuch as I could see from the stand point of an ordinary sitter in the circle, and at the same time watch my own sensations and observe from the standpoint of the medium. The facts learned under these circumstances were to me very valuable.

On one occasion, the last séance before I proceeded on my sketching tour, I was able to record in my diary the whole of my thoughts, impressions and feelings, and as it is a fairly good illustration of what a medium feels during a materialisation séance, if he or she is conscious of anything, I give it exactly as I then recorded it in my journal:—

"We reach Christiania in good time and go to get a cup of tea before proceeding to the séance room.

"My spirits go down to zero and my nervousness increases as the time draws near.

'You don't look Very happy,' remarks Janey.

'Neither do I feel so,' I reply, though I reproach myself instantly, when I remember how much trouble they have all taken to insure my comfort, and the success of the forthcoming séance, and I try to look a little less like a martyr, as I drink my tea and listen to the remarks as to the arrangements for the evening.

"When we reach the séance room I am met by several old acquaintances and I see the two little children are there again, with another little boy, son of Mrs. Pettersson, the medium.

"I feel a good deal comforted by the sight of the children. They are dear little things. They bring their stools and sit down on either side of me as a matter of course, chatting to each other and to me like a small pair of magpies.

"The gas is turned down leaving sufficient light to see every object in the room, and I can see the time by the not very clear clock at the far end. I think it is too light, but there is no need to suggest a change till it is necessary. Somebody gives me two parcels of confectionary, but, as usual during a séance, I cannot bear to have to take charge of anything; even the care of these two parcels is too much, so I hand them to my nearest neighbour together with my gloves.

"Little Jonte gets one parcel with instructions to give some of its contents to his little spirit brother, Gustav, should he come.

"Getting rid of my encumbrances, I settle down quietly, taking hold of each child's hand. It occurs to me, though, that perhaps by doing so I may in some way use up the children's strength, so I loosen my hold on them, for the little creatures need all the strength they possess.

"We sat sometime without anything occurring, though it was evident something was moving inside the cabinet behind me. We could value the good singing, which served to distract attention from the cabinet and interest one during the long interval of waiting.

"The light was lowered, and instantly a figure came from behind the curtains with such suddenness as to startle everyone.

"This was followed by a smaller one who walked round me and came to little Jonte, who at once handed it the parcel of sweets saying:——'This is for you, dear little Gustav.'

"The little white figure came back, holding the parcel and with quick eager fingers opened the paper, and reached it out to little Maja, who took some of the contents; then it poured some on to my knee and pushed them towards Jonte, who was watching anxiously for his share.

'Is it your brother, Jonte? Is it Gustav?' cried a voice from a little distance. 'Tell me, is it Gustav?'

'Yes it's Gustav,' replied Jonte with his mouth full of chocolate creams.

'Go, little Gustav,' he continued, 'and see Mamma, and give her some also,' continued he. 'Come I'll take you. You need not be afraid. I'll take care of you.'

"But Gustav went without help and poured the remainder of the contents of the parcel on his mother's knee, stroked her face with his tiny hands and drew himself back to his former place beside his brother and sister.

'Go and see Papa, little Gustav. Go my little one, he wants you,' pleaded the mother who seemed to be much agitated. But Gustav did not heed her; he remained a few minutes longer with the children, then slowly melted into air, and was gone.

"During this time another figure at my left had made its appearance several times without succeeding in coming fairly out, a tall, fully developed figure who walked with quick steps out into the middle of the circle and was there met by Mr. Lund, who rose up from his place to meet it.

"I do not know who it was nor did I remember to ask afterwards.

"This figure causes some surprise in the circle, for up to now the forms have had a muffled-up sort of appearance and a shy shrinking manner, but this one walks as though doing us a favor by coming in our midst. It brushes past me as if I did not exist and I fancy I feel a little crushed. A minute before, I was apparently the most important person in the room; now I am nobody. I feel rather curious about the looks of this stately personage, but her back is to me, and I can only judge by the figure which seems very tall, and I notice that, as she stands beside Mr Lund, she is not much shorter than he is. She walks back in the same dignified manner as before. I feel very much like reminding her that she ought to be obliged to me, and take some notice of me sitting there, instead of sweeping past in so unceremonious a fashion; but now she is gone and I have not had courage to assert myself. I feel curiously weak and powerless and can only feel without having strength to act.

"Now comes another figure, shorter, slenderer, and with outstretched arms. Somebody rises up at the far end of the circle and comes forward and the two are clasped in each others arms. Then inarticulate cries of Anna! Oh, Anna! My child! My loved one!

"Then somebody else gets up and puts her arms round the figure; then sobs, cries, and blessings get mixed up. I feel my body swayed to and fro and all gets dark before my eyes. I feel somebody's arms round me although I sit on my chair alone. I feel somebody's heart beating against my breast. I feel that something is happening. No one is near me except the two children. No one is taking any notice of me. All eyes and thoughts seem concentrated on the white slender figure standing there with the arms of the two black-robed women around it.

"It must be my own heart I feel beating so distinctly. Yet those arms round me? Surely never did I feel a touch so plainly. I begin to wonder which is I. Am I the white figure or am I the one on the chair? Are they my hands round the old lady's neck, or are these mine that are lying on the knees of me, or on the knees of the figure if it be not I, on the chair?

"Certainly they are my lips that are being kissed. It is my face that is wet with the tears which these good women are shedding so plentifully. Yet how can it be? It is a horrible feeling, thus losing hold of one's identity. I long to put out one of these hands that are lying so helplessly, and touch some one just to know if I am myself or only a dream—if 'Anna' be I, and I am lost as it were, in her identity.

"I feel the old lady's trembling arms, the kisses, the tears, the blessings and caresses of the sister, and I wonder in an agony of suspense and bewilderment, how long can it last? How long will there be two of us? Which will it be in the end? Shall I be 'Anna' or 'Anna' be I?

"Then I feel two little hands slip themselves into my nerveless ones and they give me a fresh hold of myself as it were, and with a feeling of exultation I find *I am* myself, and that little Jonte, tired of being hidden behind the three figures, feels lonely and grasps my hands for company and comfort.

"How glad I am of a touch, even from the hand of a child. My doubts as to who I am and where I am, are gone. While I am feeling thus the white figure of 'Anna' disappears in the cabinet, and the two ladies return to their seats, excited and tearful but overcome with happiness."

There was a great deal more to happen that night, but somehow I felt weak and indifferent to all around me, and not inclined to be interested in what occurred. Strange and remarkable incidents took place but for the moment my life seemed dragged out of me and I longed for solitude and rest. I ardently wished for repose far away from any city, and once the séance was over my thoughts were on the long wished for holiday. I soon recuperated and in a couple of days left for the mountains.

The remembrance of the strange sensations which overwhelmed me during the interview of "Anna" and her friends tormented me cruelly. In vain I tried to escape my own thoughts, and turn my attention to the magnificent landscapes by which I was surrounded. They pursued me, forced themselves upon me, till in self-defence I was obliged to make a stand and examine them as they presented themselves. Thoughts of incomprehensible occurrences, which had been put aside long ago, now raised themselves afresh and demanded explanation. The memory of Yolande's seizure, of many incidents which had perhaps escaped the notice of any other than myself, stood ranged before me in formidable line, and I felt that till these things were explained I could go no further.

———

CHAPTER XXV.

FROM DARKNESS TO LIGHT.

"Above the darksome sea of death
Looms the great life that is to be,
A land of cloud and mystery
A dim mirage, with shapes of men
Long dead, and passed beyond our ken."

LONGFELLOW

FOR some months after my experiences in Norway I was worried by speculations concerning spiritualistic phenomena, and some works which I had read kept the subject alive. Many times I took in review all the unexplained occurrences, all the arguments brought to bear on the origin of spirit manifestations, and weighed them in the balance with my experiences as a counterweight.

That manifestations were genuine could not be doubted, but *whence* came they? This was the question. Were these materialised forms in which I had been so interested my "subliminal consciousness" acting independently of my will, or could it possibly be the old long-feared enemy of mankind, the Devil seeking to delude us by wearing the garb of long lost friends to draw us into an abyss of iniquity and deception. Had I all these years been serving him and leading others into wrong-doing? Had my life been a series of mistakes? Would those whose eyes I had tried to open to living facts curse me for having led them from the right path?

The thought was an awful and ever present one, but I was afraid of knowing the truth. I had not courage enough to face it if so be that *that* was the truth. Better uncertainty than confirmation of that fear.

I remembered the faith of my childhood and girlhood in the loving-kindness of God and how, when I claimed the help which had been promised to all who believed, the help was not forthcoming; how I had felt then that I had built my hopes on sand and had no solid ground on which to rebuild the shattered edifice; and now this too had failed. It was the same dreary experience over again; I had nowhere to place my feet. Life was hateful; and death a fearful ending to a meaningless existence of trial and suffering.

I could understand how it was that a medium recanted and confessed that spiritualistic manifestations were only a horrible farce and deception. If my doubts and fears were confirmed it was the only honest course open for me also and I must do as others had done before me. It would be worse than death; therefore I would wait, I would know the truth, I would solve the terrible doubts let the cost be what it would. Then, should it be that I had been deceived and deceived others, I would not die till I had tried to undo by every means in my power the wrong I had wrought.

This resolution made, I had at least one thing left to live for, and began immediately to project plans for carrying out experiments. I would ignore the fact that I was a medium; I would act as though my personality was to be suspected; I would not trust myself. Experiments should be carried out to prove what part I played in the production of these manifestations; I would not trust my thoughts, my feelings, nor my own senses. If I had any part in representing the spirit forms I must know it.

I had always maintained that, neither consciously nor unconsciously, had I any part in these, beyond lending my strength, since, seeing that I never lost consciousness, it could not be. Still the devil can have many resources, and he can perhaps make me *think* I have never lost my powers of reasoning. So I argued with myself.

Having made up my mind to solve what seemed to be a question of vital importance, I felt my courage return, and from wishing that life might soon be at an end, when I might rest or at least find peace in the grave, I began to fear that death might come before I had finished my task, and I was anxious to set to work.

An attack of illness, caused perhaps by the wearing anxiety, coupled with an accidental cold, stopped all question of experiments, and when the doctor expressed a doubt as to my ultimate recovery I experienced a feeling of relief that by death I should escape both the work and the humiliation, and felt a kind of triumph in the thought that I should be prevented from carrying out my resolution in spite of myself. I took credit for the self-sacrifice I had resolved on, but inwardly rejoiced that death should take the matter in his own hands and settle the question without consulting my wishes, and I should be free. There would at least be an end of doubt, as far as I myself was concerned. I should know if spirit communication and manifestation were true. If they were not then I should be spared the humiliation of confessing to my wrong-doing. But if they were true! And if for some reason I could not return to proclaim the truth! Well, then, there would be nothing to confess. Any way I should escape the task I had set myself and could let others find out for themselves.

Now came the thought that this way of reasoning was selfish and cowardly. If I had led others wrong I must at all hazards try to undo the mischief. If I died, I lost the opportunity. To be glad to die in order to shuffle out of a self-imposed task was weak and mean. I had no right to leave the work of restitution to others. No! I must do the work myself and prove the truth or falseness of this great subject. Whether true or false I must not shrink to make it known.

I began to recover. I *must* get well. I could do nothing while sick, and I was losing valuable time. I begrudged the hours and days as they fled past till I should be able to attend to my usual duties.

It was a Sunday morning, a bright summer day. I had thrown myself on my sofa with a book, but my mind was occupied with projects as to the practical carrying out of tests, so that I did not pay much attention to its pages. I felt a curiously faint sinking sensation, and the printed pages I had been trying to study became strangely indistinct. Was I going to faint? Everything became dark and I felt sure I was going to be ill again. I would call someone, but I remembered there was no one on that side of the house.

The faintness passed away almost immediately, and I was glad I had not disturbed anyone. I glanced at my book; strange, how far away and dim it seemed. I had moved I away from the sofa, but somebody else was, there and held the book! Who could it be? How wonderfully light and strong I felt. The faintness had gone and in its place had come a marvellous sense of health, strength, and power which I had never before known.

Life was waking up within me, springing, bubbling, coursing through my veins like electric streams. Every part of my body was glowing with new vigor, and a sense of absolute untrammeled freedom. For the first time I knew what it was to live.

How strange! The room looked so small, so cramped, so dark and that dim figure on the sofa? Who was she? I seemed to recognise something in the quiet form, some faint recollection of having known her, but this irresistible sense of freedom must be indulged; I could not stay in this place, but where should I go? I moved towards the window. Strange how curiously dim my surroundings seemed. The walls appeared to approach me, to disappear; but whither I could not tell.

This phenomenon did not greatly surprise me, though I wondered somewhat, for there away a little distance off, I saw a friend whom I recognised, not as one usually recognises friends through familiarity with face or figure. Even at this moment I could not explain, nor say if he had a single familiar feature. All I knew was, he was my friend and had been my friend through ages—a friend, better, wiser, stronger than myself. I needed a friend and the friend had come. He spoke, or perhaps he did not use language though I understood better than any tongue could explain.

"Did I see where I was?"

Yes, I could see, though curiously enough the sunshine had faded and we were in a narrow road, not a pleasant one either, and as I looked around me I held my friend by the hand and felt assured of safety. It was a strange place, yet there was a curious familiarity about it. Dark gloomy overhanging rocks were on each side, obstructed here and there by projections which seemed to block up the passage. The ground was strewn with rough stones and tangled brushwood, with here and there deep holes into which unwary travellers must stumble. My eyes searched as it were gropingly along the road, inch by inch, foot by foot, an apparently insurmountable obstacle was reached, and, as I came near it I was conscious of a feeling of exultation for the difficulties shrank as I stepped forward and passed them with ease.

A pitfall yawned open-mouthed, in my pathway, and dismayed, I saw no hope of avoiding a disastrous fall into the miry depths, I looked boldy forward and as I advanced a narrow track was visible. If I did not turn dizzy, and could step firmly and carefully the gulf might be safely passed.

It was a long weary way and though I was with a friend now it was only for a short time, but I was not afraid, for though it was dark and cheerless, surrounded by cold mist that chilled the blood, and damped the courage, yet here and there gleamed out a warm clear light which filled the heart with joy and thankfulness.

Looking backwards along the road, I felt a curious sense of proprietorship. The light which had come in transient gleams seemed to have diffused itself over the whole, and I could see my footprints over its length where I had diverged from the road, wherever I had endeavoured to go around obstacles, and where I had been driven back and compelled to surmount them.

I saw the pitfalls into which I had fallen and from which I had had to drag myself painfully out again, only to find that I might have avoided the dangers had I seen the light which now lay over it all.

Looking eagerly forward again I saw the light gleaming out in the distance, while the shadows lay at our feet, and I felt a burning desire to press forward towards it, even as I felt this, a beam of light crept towards me and guided my steps.

"Can you travel the road alone?" asked my friend. "Is your courage equal to the task?"

"Yes I can if it be necessary. It is not as difficult as it looks. But I must have light, without it I should not be safe. But why should I? Are there no better roads?"

"Look farther!"

I looked farther, and, as my eyes searched, the darkness lifted itself little by little, and at the end of the road afar off a brilliant gleam of light burst out, flooding the road with glory inconceivable. I could not bear it. I was ashamed and hid my face for the light penetrated me through and through and I saw myself as I really was and not as I had in my arrogance thought myself. Could it be that others could see me as I now saw myself?

I clung to my friend and asked, "What is it? Tell me what it means."

"It is truth. It is what you have resolved to find."

"And this road, must I travel it to reach it?"

"It is the road you have made; you have no other."

"Then if I travel it, I shall find the truth. I cannot fail. I feel I cannot fail."

"You have found it already. You have only to grasp it and hold it close."

"Help me, let me see more, teach me to understand. How shall I reach it, how hold it fast."

"You have reached it; you have seen it before, but you did not recognise it. It has lighted your pathway but you would not acknowledge it."

"It has been so faint, so dim, I did not know," I said humbly.

"You have felt it, but you put it aside, and raised barriers between it and you, and hid it from your sight."

"I did not know, I did not know."

"You closed your eyes and walked blindly into snares and pitfalls; you preferred to trust to your fancied wisdom rather than to the light; you turned aside for new paths which led away from it."

"I did not know, I did not know."

"You had the light within your grasp. You saw it gleaming, but it offended you because it discovered things which were offensive to you. You preferred to let darkness cover them out of sight and tried to believe they did not exist. You cast the light behind you and walked on into darkness and despair."

"I did not know, I did not know."

"You thought in your heart: 'I am sufficient unto myself. I will do this thing, I will do that thing,' and so you stumbled, fell into the mire, and when you were baffled at every turn, you turned back, thwarted in your plans, deceived by your own desire; then and only then you asked for truth."

"I did not know; help me to understand truth, to hold fast to it. Help me to approach this wonderful light; let me understand the meaning of life. I will not let you go. Oh help me, help me!"

I clung to my friend. We turned aside from the contemplation of the road. A sense of motion, bewilderment, increasing light, intense living radiance, and then—Who can describe the indescribable? Time had disappeared, space was no longer existing. I was overpowered by my own insignificance. How mean, how small an atom I was of this unutterable greatness; yet one with it, born of it, belonging to it. I realised this, even with my sense of smallness, and knew that, mean and poor as I was, I was yet a part of this undying, infinite, indestructible whole; that without me it would not be complete.

The light of this great life penetrated me, and I understood,—*understood that thoughts were the only real tangible substances*, and why, between my friend and me, utterance was not needed. The secrets of life and death were unveiled and the meaning became plain. The reason of sin and suffering, the everlasting struggle towards perfection were evident; how each atom of life had its appointed place into which it fitted as no other atom could; how each change and evolution brought it nearer to its goal. As desire arose within me I found the means of grasping it. Knowledge was mine. I had only to desire and it was in my grasp.

And I had dared to doubt, dared to question the power of God,—nay, his very existence! I had presumed to question the fact of spiritual life. I had blindly called the dark shadowy confines of earthly existence the real life.

I stood with my friend, overcome with this new sense of reality, this wonderful truth. I saw other beings, living radiant creatures, and felt humbled and ashamed of my own inferiority; yet my soul went out to them in love, friendship, and adoration. I longed for their friendship and their love.

What was this? My longing went out from me as a stream of silvery light. It reached them; a line, a cord of communication, born of my very desire. I could go to them, they could come to me; they were conscious of the aspiration, smiled on me, and I felt that I had been blessed beyond my deserts.

There were others for whom I felt an intense compassion and an irresistible desire to draw them nearer to me. They might come if they would, they might approach me did they desire it. They could come to me, even as I could come nearer those bright creatures of love and truth. If they would only let me, I could do so much to dispel the shadows in which they were surrounded.

They had helped me, made themselves one with me. We had worked together. We had at times succeeded, at times failed; we had been baffled by difficulties, had fallen headlong into snares; in all we had been together. We had worked without light, but they bore their share as I did; we were equally weak, equally blind, equally guilty.

What was the difference now? Why did I pity them? Why wish to draw them nearer to me? I was no better than they, no higher. No! there was no better, no worse, no higher, no lower. We were all the same; all members of the great family, all atoms of one great creative soul; but I, the atom less wise, less clever, than those whom I pitied, had found the light which they were yet seeking.

The light had entered my soul and I was filled with joy ineffable. It was mine, this new born fire. It could not escape through all eternity. It was within their hands too, but they had not laid hold of it. It was round about them, within them; but they were not conscious of it. They were in the same position as I when on the road. I would teach them. I would help them. I would show them how to grasp the truth and hug it to them, help them as my friend had helped me into the light. They would understand, even as I did, what this great light and love meant. If they would only send out one little desire to me for my help.

I stretched out my arms, cried to them. I felt my whole being filled with an aching yearning to lift them to me. How easily I could do it. How easily they could partake of this glorious new life if they would.

How could I attract their attention? How show them the way? Oh! for some of the radiant beauty of those glorious beings whose smile had blessed me. Oh! for a little of the light and influence they shed on my way. I would seek them, for they would help me. I would drink in this living glorious truth, it should fill my whole being, that I in turn might reflect its glory on those I loved and for whom I had such great compassion. My whole consciousness resolved itself into the prayer: "Help me that I may help others."

CHAPTER XXVI.

THE MYSTERY SOLVED.

"Thus the Seer,
With vision clear,
Sees forms appear and disappear,
In the perpetual round of strange,
Mysterious change
From birth to death, from death to birth.
From earth to heaven, from heaven to earth;
Till glimpses more sublime
Of things, unseen before,
Unto his wondering eyes reveal
The Universe, as an immeasurable wheel
Turning for evermore
In the rapid and rushing river of Time."

LONGFELLOW

As THE desire was formed, it filled and animated every fibre of my being, throbbed and pulsated, gathering strength and energy till action was irresistible, and I felt strong to understand, and strong to begin the work which had suddenly become for me the great animating principle of happiness.

To teach others, I must learn myself. But where begin? It surprised me to find how difficult it was to remember what special subject it was that had troubled me to understand. It was with a feeling akin to pain that I searched within myself for some clue to what had puzzled me and made me unhappy. It was so long ago, or in some way it seemed related to some half forgotten dream; the feeling of unsatisfaction was clear, but how had it arisen? It resembled the sense of depression which a sleeper experiences on awakening from some uncomfortable dream, while he is unable to recall the vision which gave birth to the feeling. That I had dreamed of a state of existence which differed in some way from this, I knew, and I also knew that I must recall the dream in order to find what mystery it was I wished to solve.

Incident after incident revealed itself, as pictures which I recognised as belonging to the dream, dim, blurred and indistinct, in which I saw myself as acting a part; pictures which caused me a sense of shame and humiliation; and I hurried to let them fall into the mists of forgetfulness. One by one I was able to grasp the incidents Yet at the best it was a broken chain and its want of sequence troubled or puzzled me. I could not find anything to fill up the blanks. Had I forgotten? or had the dream been only a disconnected chain of thoughts or fancies? Who I was, what the name I bore, seemed to have no significance, nor could I recall it, but through all the dull and undefined mistiness of the dream, my own identity, the Ego which was now trying to grasp the vague threads and shadows, was the same, the only clear palpable and unmistakable fact which required no exertion to recall, and I was able to follow it little by little, step by step, through the intricacies of my strange experience. One by one, I gathered up the threads of the dream life and saw it in its entirety, saw how it had been influenced by others, how many other individualities had come in touch with it, how many conflicting sympathies and attractions had swayed and deflected its original purpose.

Interestedly as though unravelling a tangled skein I followed the threads from cause to effect, from motive to action, and I saw that the motives were pure and earnest. I saw the intense desire for knowledge and the desire for help to obtain it. I saw how this desire attracted those who from sympathy wished to help, but in these, alas, the knowledge too was wanting and the result was disaster.

My interest in the mysterious dream-life drew me involuntarily downwards or upwards—it matters not which, since there exists neither the one nor the other,—but nearer to a misty cloudlike region in which one felt stifled, cramped as though the atmosphere had become close, thick and substantial. A feeling of almost fear and anxiety oppressed me, and I felt an instinctive desire to escape from the sense of heaviness which was gradually closing in and around me; yet the desire to learn was stronger, and gathering all my energies I combatted the instinct which would lead to clearer air and freedom.

There was a vague sense of familiarity in the vaporous mistiness, something in the forms and shapes which recalled the dream-life more vividly, and gradually I became aware that in this region the dream-life was lived. I saw that all this misty world was teeming with life, real life—struggling individualities, each with aims, ambitions, hopes, fears, joys, despairs, strangely alike, yet different; each seemingly existing of itself, yet each dependent on the other, each influencing, leading, attracting, or repelling each other.

Viewed from my point of observation it would seem that this world of mist was evolving from itself a living something, which would rise up, perfected and purified, into the world of reality, and in this something I recognized the spirit of humanity akin to those perfect beings whom I had so lately seen.

As I recognized this, the fear of the misty world gave place to a lively sympathy and interest, I knew that it was the world in which the incidents of the dream-life were enacted, but I wondered how it was that objects were so different. These rocks, these seas which had before seemed so solid, so unfathomable were only vapours or clouds, through which I passed without resistance. They offered no opposition to my progress. I passed as easily as an arrow through the clouds, and came in closer contact with the human spirits I had seen from afar.

Curiously they were unconscious of my nearness. They passed me by without seeing me; they took no notice of my friendly advances; they seemed each intent on his own thoughts which revolved round and round the central point—the ego of each individuality; never losing sight of it, all striving one with the other for the purpose of increasing its importance.

How blindly, how mistakenly they were working, these strugglers, driven by that, to them, mysterious force, to develope, to improve, to become greater and more excellent, to rise above the level of their surroundings. They obeyed the instinct, but shutting their eyes to the light, they laboured blindly and gropingly, accumulating stores which they believed would raise them above their fellows, but they buried themselves under them instead. They obeyed the instinct which impelled them onward to develope themselves into something better and greater than before; yet they were without the knowledge of how to apply their possessions to their advantage and the furtherance of their desires. They worked with energy as though the dream-life were the whole—the Alpha and Omega—of existence, yet knowing that dissolution would unquestionably overtake them. Oh! if they could only see the light through which I saw, and know what this great impulse, this instinct meant, and how they misunderstood it, they would hasten to repair the mistakes they were committing. They believed in death yet worked as though they did not. I felt an infinite pity and compassion for these mistaken ones, and was thrilled with a desire to show them my treasure which I had found and which was to me the key to all the secrets of this wonderful existence. Through it I saw that this life which animates all things is undying, immortal; that there is no death, no annihilation; that it is the same life which circling for ever and ever through form after form, dwelling in the rocks, the sand, the sea, in each blade of grass, each tree, each flower, in all forms of animal existence, culminates in Man's intelligence and perception. Through it I saw that all events, all progress, movements, revolutions, are but the expression of obedience to the laws which govern the universe, and that the movements which had seemingly been organised and carried out by men of their own free-will, had in fact been brought about by natural laws from which there is no escape; the individual whose intelligence most quickly perceived and appreciated the necessity of action becoming for the time a leader of his fellows.

I could understand that, for the development of intelligence and perception, the spirit must pass through all organisms, gathering qualifications and properties incident to and peculiar to each; that the spirit and intelligence of man were the outcome and accumulation of all the knowledge gathered during an infinitude of existences in different forms and conditions which must go on and on for ever. I could see that the fact of the spirit first taking on itself the form of man did not bring it to its utmost earthly perfection, for there are many degrees of men. In the savage it widens its experience, and finds a new field for education, which being exhausted, another step is taken; and so, step by step, in an ever onward, progressive, expansive direction, the spirit developes, the decay of the forms which the spirit employs being only the evidence that they have fulfilled their mission and served the purpose for which they were used. They return to their original elements to be used again and again as a means whereby the spirit can manifest itself and obtain the development it requires..

All this I saw so plainly; it seemed so simple, so rational, so complete, that I wondered how it was I had not known it before. Where had my senses been that I had been unable to see these simple things? Only now by the aid of my new treasure, were the laws made visible.

How I longed to bring this light to bear on all the shadowy places, all the darknesses, which lay before me in this mysterious unreal life in which so many were struggling blindly, not knowing why they strove. I remembered my own distress, my own anxieties, desires and wish for enlightenment. They seemed so petty and trivial now compared with the great need I saw, that I was loath to constrain my thoughts to any contemplation of personal interest. I was no longer afraid of what truth might reveal. The light had already become so dear, so precious to me that come what might I would never let it go. Already it had shown me the great deficiencies, faults, and weaknesses in myself, and the possibilities which ought to have been cultivated. It had shown me what life is, and what it might become, and I knew that with the aid of this great holy light, all things might be made plain, all darkness made light, all secret things discovered.

The longing desire to help these blind ones became more intense, more irresistible, but they did not see me, did not heed me, and I strove in vain to make myself understood. I reached out my hands but they passed by; I called out but they were intent on other things and did not hear me. Then I became aware that to come within the ken of these spirits I too must clothe myself with mist. It was a repugnant thought, yet to help them I would do it. But how? This question formed itself and in a flash I recognised that this was the object of my search, and which had only been present as a vague undefined longing.

The longing had brought me from a world of radiant light, where love and sympathy alone existed, had brought me to this dim shadowy world of unrealities to which the light could scarcely penetrate. It was here the knowledge must be gained. I must learn how to clothe myself with this mist, this material so immaterial, so vague; how to manipulate and fashion it; how to take hold of and grasp that which has no substance. It appeared impossible, yet I saw that it had been done. A long time I searched for means to carry my desire into execution; then some one came to my aid, and together we considered how this thing was to be accomplished. In answer to my query how to hold together this immaterial substance, he showed me how, by sweeping together masses of the cloudy mists, by breathing into it the life with which I was myself endowed, forcing into it, by my will, part of my own desire and intensity of purpose it became animated with part of myself, condensed, grew in form, as the shadowy misty beings around me, unconscious of my existence. It was my own creation, my own special property, animated with my life, held in existence by my will, obedient to my wish or command, dependent on me for each moment of its being. Did the intensity of my will relax, did my desire or interest waver one iota, I knew this shadowy likeness of myself must return to the mist from which it came and cease to exist.

Yet to those children of the mist, this creation of mine was real, tangible as themselves, not wanting in life nor intelligence. It was only *I* who was conscious of the fact that it was only the shadow of the reality, wanting in many things which I was too inexperienced to impart to it. Yet what possibilities might await on further experience, with what properties, might I not endow this shadowy creation when I had learned my own powers! Truly I had solved the mystery. Yet only one part of it, some other way some other means had surely been used?

Now with the help of my friend we together called into being, a weird shadow which was neither of us, only an unshapen, unformed thing, which we, with infinite pains, tried to fashion into shape; but our wills and sense of fitness of things did not accord, and the result was failure. The shadow we had together created from the mist was wanting in many respects, and we endeavoured to fill up the deficiencies, to repair the faults, to make the shadow as the one previously,—a counterpart of a living reality,—yet notwithstanding our efforts, we failed and in spite of the desire to call into shape a creature resembling the first, we could at best only build up a miserable conterfeit which could not be animated because of the conflicting wills of its creators.

This then was the mystery. And I felt a sense of fiery shame and humiliation. I had blamed my friend for failure which I had helped to bring about. I had brought my will into the work of creation and the ideas crossed each other as the lines of two wet drawings laid face to face become crossed, blotted, effaced, and unrecognisable.

Energy misdirected, ungoverned by reason and knowledge, must fail in achieving the purpose intended, and so it was with us.

The mystery was a mystery no longer, and I longed to express contrition for the unkindness I had felt for my friend; how sorry I was; how I wished to make amends, and help instead of blaming. I saw it was I who had led the way into error by my will and wish to attain an end to which my strength was not sufficient.

As I pondered on these things the sorrows and anxieties which had ruffled the even tenor of the dream-life came more home to me, and I remembered many half forgotten joys and sorrows, which had once been realities, speculations as to another life, another existence outside of the dream, and I felt an amused pity for the ignorance of the dreamer, who could mistake the dream-life for the glorious reality.

Now that I had solved the problem it seemed my work was done. I knew now how I could approach these struggling benighted ones, and I would help them with all my strength. I would show them the light by which they would see the right road to knowledge. I would not weary with teaching, but now I was free to leave this shadowy region, free to once more breathe the bright lighted air I had left, to drink in the beauty of that other world and enjoy the inexpressible love and affection which emanated from and actuated its people.

I would come back to these people of the mists, but first let me gather fresh strength and courage from those radiant beings whose smile had warmed and thrilled me with an extasy of love and veneration. Yet a strange sensation as of some great attraction kept me, and in vain I tried to shake myself free from its influence. I wanted freedom, liberty; yet I was like a captive being drawn back to the prison from whence he had escaped. I knew that, resist as I would, I must obey the power which was impelling me; so grasping with all my strength the treasure I had found I obeyed, and sorrowfully, yet elate because of my treasure, I found my former home in the shadow land.

As when I left, the walls appeared to approach and recede. I passed through as through a mist, and stood with the same sense of unreality, looking at the woman lying still, book in hand, either sleeping or dead. That this woman's form was the prison from which I had escaped I knew now, and that I must again become captive. I knew that I must submit; there was so much for me to do to show these poor struggling spirits that beyond the shadows there is a living reality, absolute and perfect, that the treasure I had grasped might also be theirs, to help them on the way to freedom. Only clothed in these misty garments, could I approach them and tell them these things; so I was content to return, and wait patiently for the time of release, knowing my duty and glad to do it.

The same sense of pain, of faintness and weary depression, and again I was conscious of lying on my couch, book in hand. I opened my eyes; all about me was the same, nothing was changed; the flowers, the pictures, the curtains were as they had always been; but there was this great change, that I had withal a sense of joy, rest and absolute content, such as I had never known before.

How long I had been away I have no knowledge, for in the world of reality I had visited, time is not, nor space, nor anything by which to measure as on the earth.

Strange how the shadow and the reality change places. Had I not known better I should have said that earthly scenes were the realities and the world I had visited the dream-world. But the treasure I had found there is still in my grasp. This one atom of the living truth has brought me that Peace which passeth all understanding, and by its clear light I see and know that spirit communication is true; true as that God lives.

They may say I dreamed, but it matters not, for I know that it was no dream but a foretaste of life, real and indisputable; and that during the remainder of my journey through the shadows it will help me to bear with patience whatever may befall, and give me courage to fight to the end.

———

CHAPTER XXVII.

SPIRIT PHOTOGRAPHS?

"As thou knowest not what is the way of the spirit,…even so thou knowest not the works of God who maketh all."

ECCLESIASTES, CH. N. V. 5

I HAD not been long acquainted with the subject of spiritualism when the question arose as to the possibility of obtaining photos of the unseen—transcendental, occult, or spirit photographs, whatever we may call them. I had not then realized how much I suffered from séances or how great was the drain upon the vitality caused by them. My health not being at any time very robust, it did not occur to me that my weariness and utter exhaustion could be ascribed to some of those with whom I came in contact at the séances. My friends were continually proposing experiments, which as a rule were quite as interesting to me as to them, and amongst others the idea of obtaining spirit photos incessantly cropped up. I was anxious that every opportunity should be utilised but not being a photographer myself there was no system or continued effort, in our experiments in this direction, and we did not then understand how difficult it is to have various forms of mediumship equally developed at one and the same time without overstraining the nervous system.

In any case, although I tried for the desired photos whenever I had the chance, it was not until 1876 when in London that I supposed I had been successful; and even then I did not ascribe the result to my mediumship.

Mrs Burns who is herself a highly gifted sensitive went with me to the spirit photographer, Mr. Hudson. After being photographed, Mr. H. developed the plate and was quite elated with the success that had attended my visit, as a very beautiful figure had come on the plate beside my photo. He hurried into the room with the welcome news delighted to show me the plate, when his foot caught in the mat and the plate was dashed to pieces.

Shortly afterwards I visited Paris and Brussells. At the latter place I was photographed one forenoon no fewer than twenty times without obtaining the slightest symptom of what we were aiming at.

I do not remember any more persistent efforts being made for a couple of years, although now and again we tried when an opportunity offered itself. Between 1878 and 1880 various photographers attempted without being successful.

In 1880 when I went to Sweden I took with me a camera and 288 plates, which I used, hoping that at sometime we should see a glimpse of what we desired. I obtained assistance from a photographer, and went on with the work more systematically than on any previous occasion, but my health was not restored for nearly seven years after the terrible shock from the séance in Newcastle in 1880, so that my mediumship for the time being was almost nil. When the 24 dozen plates had been used the camera was neglected and ultimately damaged.

In 1888, 1889 and 1890 several attempts were made, and one solitary photograph was quite unexpectedly obtained in the latter year at villa O. P. in Gothenburg as before described, when I sat for Mr. Boutlerof to see if the camera was properly focussed, and to test the magnesium light which had been arranged. Mr. Aksakof, and some other of my friends were discussing the subject of spirit photos when Mr. Boutlerof interrupted the conversation by coming in and saying:—

"I have the camera focussed for the chair in the corner of the other room and I want you Mrs. E., to come and sit for me, so that I may try the light."

This was in the twilight of the evening just before lighting the lamps. We all rose from our seats and accompanied Mr. Boutlerof into the room where the camera was standing. There was no order or arrangement as to where we should sit except that I was told to "take the chair in the corner." I did so and the magnesium light was immediately flashed, when all present saw

One of the first shadow forms.
(Photographed 3 p. m. 8 Febr. 1897).

Shadow form photographed 3 p. m. 9 Febr. 1897.

the figure of a man standing behind me. This form was not visible before or after the flash, and all were curious to see whether he had made any impression on the plate. Fortunately his photo had been secured.

At intervals we tried in Gothenburg, Christiania, Berlin and other places, but still without success.

In 1896 I went to England and whilst there obtained some, to me, doubtful manifestations of what were supposed to be spirit photographs. For various reasons which I need not now enter upon I did not feel able to accept them as genuine, although they may have been so.

I thereupon decided to have another trial on my return to Germany. I carried out my intention and obtained several cloudy, indistinct forms of invisible objects, but I became so extremely nervous that I had to give up the photographing for two or three weeks. Then I tried again and obtained clearer figures of the unseen. Two or three were excellent portraits of what appeared to be ordinary living human beings. Again my nerves troubled me so much, that I dared not venture to go down-stairs; in fact I scarcely had courage to walk across the room, so that the experiments had to cease.

In January 1897 I went to Gothenburg for a couple of months intending to get the manuscript of this book ready for the printer. My friends bought a new camera and all the necessary outfit for the purpose of a new series of experiments in spirit photography. On the 28th of January they had all in order for this new study. As they had not previously given any attention to the subject of photography they had much to learn. The first three days were a kind of preliminary experimental time, in order to get a little accustomed to the camera, focussing, developing, printing, and so forth.

On the 1st of February we began the work systematically, but failures were all that we had to report. We had, however, decided to continue the work whatever the result, provided my health did not give way or some other unsurmountable obstacle present itself.

On the 2nd of February when one of the exposed plates had been developed, a very slight cloudy form was perceptible. We were uncertain whether to attach any value to it as the precursor of something more decided and clear.

Next day there was a head on one of the plates. The features and general outline reminded us of our old and dear friend Georgio who had died several years ago.

On the 4th and 5th we got a slight indication of a form of some kind. On the 6th all the plates exposed were failures, but on the 7th there was perceptible a kind of mistiness like that of a head.

On the 8th and 9th two very distinct cloud-like forms of human beings appeared on the plates. No features or clear outlines were visible—the figures reminded one somewhat of forms made of snow. These, however, were so distinct as to give us encouragement to continue.

The two following days, 10th and 11th, all the plates exposed were failures. We then began to devise means of improving our methods of work. We decided to try and arrange the light for a shorter exposure, because some days, when the sky was overcast or snow was falling, we had varied the exposure from 40 to 100 seconds. Sometimes we had photographed in the morning and sometimes in the afternoon, but henceforth we decided to begin punctually at three o'clock in the afternoon, no matter what the weather might be. Another important decision was to use on dull days a magnesium flash light so as to shorten the exposure.

Hitherto the photographing had been conducted in a corner sitting-room facing south and west. This we could not improve upon. We had also used a dark brown screen as a background. This, too, we decided we could not improve, unless we covered it with black cloth so that any white form might be all the more visible. We were usually five in all who took part in the experiments, namely my host, his wife, their two daughters and myself. When the clock struck three we all entered the sitting-room. One of us placed the screen in position, another looked after the camera, whilst a third sat beside the screen so as to get the right focus. Another looked after the Venetian blinds and arranged

Y-Ay-Ali photographed at 3 p. m. 12 Febr. 1897.
Lily F. sitter.

Spirit photo obtained 12 Febr. 1897. Supposed to be portrait of Yolande (the younger).

them to give the best light effect. We all took turns in attending to the camera, and when we at last had got the magnesium apparatus to work properly, we made all ready and waited in silence 30 seconds, exposed the plate five seconds, and then flashed the magnesium light. Sometimes we took three or four and sometimes six or seven photos. Immediately they were taken we went into the dark room and developed them. We had now worked about a fortnight and were again beginning to seriously discuss other, and what might possibly be better, modes of procedure.

On the 12th however we were rewarded with two figures, the features of one being quite distinct. This gave us considerable encouragement. Next day all were failures again.

On the 14th two faces were obtained. One was supposed to bear some resemblance to my hosts mother. The other reminded us of Huss, or some one whose portrait we might possibly have seen, but who apparently, judging from his dress, had lived in the middle ages. On the following Tuesday we were surprised to find the daily newspapers had articles describing the life work of Philip Melancthon who was born 16th Febr. 1497 and we then recognised the resemblance between the photo we had obtained and the portrait of Melancthon.

On the 15th and 16th all were failures. This we were not surprised at as I had caught a severe cold after a hot bath. However, we continued our experiments all the same.

On the 17th we exposed several plates as above described and obtained a beautiful form of the invisibles. It was however only upon developing the plates that we found how far we had been successful.

On the 18th and 19th slightly misty forms of two heads appeared. On the 20th we obtained the photo of a girl supposed to be our little Spanish friend Ninia who died in Santiago in South America.

On the 21st, 22nd, 23rd, 24th and 27th we every day obtained at least one or two photos of the invisibles, and, on three occasions, when strangers had sat beside the screen. On the 25th, 26th and 28th all were failures. This for the present ended what we termed the "February experiments."

On the first of March I went to Stockholm to visit some of my friends there and was away a week. When I returned on the 8th I was very much exhausted with séances. However on the 9th we began again and continued every day up to the 15th, taking during these seven days 30 photographs, of which seven were successful. Next day, the 16th March, Mrs. and Miss F. and I left for Copenhagen. During these five weeks we had exposed in all 132 plates of which 102 had been failures.

I have had very serious doubts about the advisability of giving any details of these photographic experiments, seeing that the work was purely tentative and we had not exhausted what we considered was well within our reach. However, as the whole record of my mediumship is more or less a record of experiment, I see many objections to closing this book in silence as to this new phase of mediumship, although I object to giving the details of work which is so incomplete. The whole series of photos show that we were purely in the experimental stage, but our methods of work, and how after many years of fruitless attempts and some hundreds of failures we at last began to be successful, may be of interest to the psychical student and a sufficient reason for here recording the little we have accomplished.

In all probability I could have obtained these photos ten or twenty years ago had I worked to obtain them alone, and left other forms of mediumship in abeyance. I have no doubt whatever but that the photos are produced by spirit agency, but whether they are actual photos of spirits, or photos of what spirits have produced on the plates, I leave unsaid until I have had further opportunities of investigating.

I attach much importance to the work, and strange to say my health took no harm, but actually improved whilst the daily photographing was going on, so that I see in this a possibility of a great work being performed if we are spared to do it. Mrs. F. took an intense interest in all the details and laboured early and late at the printing, toning, and fixing of the photos, so that we all had a full share of the work, and if there was any serious loss of vitality on my part the favorable conditions enabled me to recuperate so quickly that the loss was imperceptible.

Portrait obtained 3 p. m. 14 Febr. 1897. Supposed
to be that of Philip Melancthon.

Yolande (the younger) photographed 4 p. m.
15 March 1897.

Photo supposed to be that of Ninia.
Obtained 3 p. m. 20th Febr. 1897.

Photo obtained 3 p. m. 27th Febr. 1897.
Supposed to be Elias ben Ammand of Nazarath who spent his
life amongst the lepers in Palestine.

CHAPTER XXVIII.

INVESTIGATORS I HAVE KNOWN.

"Men are enemies of that which they do not know."
Arabian Proverb

"If the bats refuse the society of the sun, does that prove
that the sun is not brilliant?"   Saadi

In glancing over the work of experiment and investigation of
the past quarter of a century, I can see into what errors one has
unconsciously fallen; errors of judgement in a great measure, but
for the most part errors caused by a blameworthy ignorance of
the simplest natural laws.

The fact that if we could produce a certain result we must
supply materials possessing the necessary qualifications, has been
too much overlooked, or perhaps we have taken it too much for
granted that those who professed an interest in the subject were
able to supply them. It is only after severe lessons, learned by
dint of much suffering, that the knowledge has been forced on
us. It would be as useless to supply a brickmaker with sand and
water expecting him to make bricks, that would stand the test of
wear, as to form a circle from the majority of so-called enquirers
and expect the spirits to produce manifestations that are beyond
all doubt. Like the brickmaker they do what they can with the
materials at their disposal, and if the results are of questionable
quality it is not their fault, but that of the persons who supplied
the material.

Most persons turning, their attention to studies of this nature, have presumably a comfortable conviction that they are
specially fitted for understanding and solving the problems pertaining to them, and they conduct their investigation in various
fashions. As a rule their manner of investigation gives the clue to

the nature of the material they place at the disposal of the unseen workers.

I have come in contact with several classes of investigators, working with a view to establishing some pet theory or other of their own. Those phenomena which would give color to, or fall in with, their preconceived theories, are eagerly seized upon to the disregard of all others that have no such bearing, or are contradictory to their ideas. These investigators are generally satisfied with theory, their imagination supplying all the rest. Hence the origin of "Spooks", "Shells", "Thought-forms," "Elementary Spirits" and similar absurdities. But even these abortive productions, of a too superficial investigation are to be preferred to the conclusions arrived at by another class of wise or scientific researchers, who begin their enquiry with the assumption that all persons except themselves are dishonest, all opinions except their own biased or without legitimate foundation, all observation except their own unreliable, all recorded phenomena unfounded unless they have witnessed them; all phenomena obtained under other conditions than those laid down by themselves unworthy of credence.

Their verdict shortly summed up amounts to this, "We have found fraud, consequently there is no truth," or in other words they might say; "Our minds can understand fraud but are unable to comprehend truth, consequently it does not exist." Reasoning in the same logical manner one might say, a false coin is a sufficient evidence to prove that there are no real ones. Other minds might argue: "if there were no true coins there would be no false ones," but not so these wise men.

There is another class, but I will do my country-men the justice of saying I have not found any among them. These act on the principle of setting a thief to catch a thief. Pretending the most fervent interest in spiritualism, they make the acquaintance of persons having the reputation of being mediums, beg as for their very lives for the privilege of assisting at a seance for experiment, simulate the warmest sympathy and friendliest feelings towards the medium, and when finally they are permitted to join the circle, take with them a camera or a member of the secret police to assist in unmasking the deception they believe to be practised.

An investigator of this class urged on by the clergy does not disdain to spy on a medium's privacy through holes which he has bored in the door or wall of his room. Or after cordially inviting a medium to pay a friendly visit to his home, he obtains false keys or picks the lock of the medium's trunk in order to examine its contents. He will induce a medium, by dint of promises and persuasion, to give a séance to a few intimate friends, and then has him or her—frequently the latter—stripped to the skin to satisfy himself that he or she does not carry on their persons, the means wherewith to deceive the innocent and unsuspecting (?) investigator. When he is satisfied on this point he ties the medium up with ropes, fastens him with screws or bolts to the wall or floor, and then awaits with complacent self-satisfaction spiritual manifestations.

My blood boils within me when I hear of sensitive mediums, frequently young girls or ladies, being subjected to the indignities and insults of these "investigators," who on the first intimation of something which to their limited understanding appears suspicious, are eager to denounce the unfortunate culprit and spread the damning news abroad, gleefully boasting of their skill as detectives. Knowing what I know—and that is little enough—of the conditions necessary for successful manifestations, I cannot but wonder greatly that success ever attends on such experiments. When the material supplied by the investigators is chiefly made up of suspicion, intrigue, and doubt, supplemented in most cases by the noxious fumes of alcohol and nicotine, what wonder that the results produced are such as bring disgrace and shame on the name of the truths they profess to advocate, and ruin to the medium, who is the victim on whom the onus of the scandal is laid?

I have heard it said that there are but few good mediums left to work for the cause. I am not surprised. They have suffered so much at the hands of ignorant investigators, who pride themselves on their special qualifications as enquirers, that they have withdrawn from the work heartsick and discouraged, weary to death of even the very name of the truths for which they have given the best they had,—time, health, reputation.

But thank God there is a brighter side. There are some good men and true, men on whom the scientific and detective investigator looks with contemptuous pity; men honest in themselves, their thoughts, and actions, who will not degrade either themselves or their neighbour by harbouring a doubt of his honesty, who prefer to believe every man innocent of evil till he is proved guilty. The innate perception of the mysterious power that rules the universe gives such a man, in this enquiry, a point of observation which others could not, by aid of all the earthly sciences, ever hope to attain. *They* may come to *believe* in a spiritual existence; *he knows it.*

He may not be learned in the classics, he may not know Greek from Latin, but compared with them he is as a skylark to a mole. While these whose interests are of the earthly pursue their occupation of pulverising and throwing up little mounds of the soil in which they find their sustenance, blind to everything on the earth above them, the bird though making his home low down on its surface can mount on light wings into the world of air and sunshine, with his joyful song of praise. Of him and such as he were the words spoken: "The pure in heart shall see God;" for so it is, that only they who have clean minds, clean bodies, and a sincere desire for light will find the truth. The man whose spirit is held in the bondage of his appetite, who clouds his brain and destroys his nerves by the poison of nicotine, or unduly excites them by the incense of wine, is no fit candidate for communion with those passed on to the world of spirit. Nor is he, who is urged on merely by the desire to substantiate some pet idea or vague dream, to establish a theory, or to aggrandize his reputation as a man of learning, or as a discoverer, any better fitted for the work. Unless a purer and better motive than these leads him on, let him not embark on the quest for he will fail. And he who seeks only to discover deceit in others, thereby betraying the falseness in himself, will find that which he seeks— falsehood; the truth he will never discover.

But to you, who are weary of life, its never ending toils, its pains, its sorrow, to you whose heart craves for certainty, to you whose dear ones have passed away leaving you despairing and heartsick, to you who hunger and thirst for proofs of a life beyond; to you I say, clean your minds from prejudice, your brain from poison, your bodies from impurities of disease wrought by the indulgence of the appetite, and set out on the search, for be assured you will find what you seek. The ground whereon you would tread is Holy; profane it not with feet soiled with the mire of suspicion, nor regard the instrument by which you must approach it as unworthy of trust. Come, honestly desiring to learn, not of the faults, failings, and shortcomings of others, but humbly seeking the truth, and you will not seek in vain; but if it be not sought with prayerful minds and earnest desire for help and enlightenment then do not waste time on the search.

"Where two or three are gathered together in my name, there am O in their midst" said the Great Teacher. Even so in these matters. Where all are met together, having duly fitted themselves for the work, where no element of suspicion is introduced, where medium and circle are seated in the presence of each other, animated by the same desire for truth; there will the manifestations be purer and better than in the old days of cabinets, cages, bonds and tests, that defeated their own purpose.

I have devoted much space to the misunderstandings, mishaps, failures, and the resulting sickness and misery attending many of the investigations. My object in giving these dark shades of the picture, when I had many brighter episodes to select from, is because I think there are more valuable lessons taught by these failures than the most brilliant successes.

There is only one more serious misfortune, at least very serious to me, which stands prominently forward and to which I have not referred. This occurred in 1893 in Helsingfors and caused my hair to turn white and grey during nearly two years of indisposition, when it all came out and with returning health grew again quite dark as it was before the accident. A full description of this remarkable séance may be had from Oswald Mutze, Leipzig, entitled "Ein seltsames und belehrendes Phänomen im Gebiete der Materialisation von Alexander N. Aksakow." (A remarkable and instructive phenomenon in materialisation.) This has also been translated into French and can be had from P. G. Leymarie, Rue du Sommerard 12, Paris. I have tried to take you my readers into my confidence and give you the result of my investigation of this strange subject. I have told you candidly my troubles during my childhood and youth as to the mysterious appearance of the "shadow-people" and how the mists of doubt were dispersed when I thought I understood what they were.

Then came our various experiments and the terrible troubles that followed some of them, so serious indeed that on three occasions my life seemed to hang as on a thread.

I have told you what in most cases others have written or published as to the phenomena, so that I do not lay claim to the statements as being entirely my own. I have used them in hopes that my experiences may be all the more easily understood, that my doubts and difficulties whilst treading new paths may be comprehended and appreciated.

I have tried to give you, as it were, an insight into my thoughts, feelings and sensations at the time; if I could have left out a description of the phenomena it is possible I would have done so, but without some record of them my doubts and perplexities would have been incomprehensible.

Much—perhaps too much—has been already written of these things and they may in consequence have fallen into disrepute. My object has not been so much to record phenomena as to use them to shew what in my case,—in my search for truth—has resulted from them.

I have used the word "medium" in the popular sense as ordinarily understood. This I have done in order that you might all the easier follow me. Now I come to the point where I wish to disclaim the right to that title. If you, my reader, have carefully followed me I think you will have come to the same conclusion as I have done on this point.

Seeing that the manifestations in all cases were in accordance with what the sitters were, it is I think self-evident that the latter were the medium and I only a part.

When the circle was composed of children the phenomena were of a childish character. When scientists were present the manifestations were of a scientific description. When ultimately I threw aside the old idea of mediums and mediumship, and determined to be no longer isolated from the rest and deprived of the use of one of my senses, I consider I took the place I ought to have occupied from the first. Even in the taking of the photographs we incessantly changed places, and had no cabinet or separate medium. We were all the medium.

In a circle of, say twenty, it is utterly absurd to credit one with the manifestations that are the product of other nineteen. When the phenomena depend on twenty why should one of the number be praised or blamed for what is produced through the whole of them?

So long as one of the circle was isolated from the rest, it was more or less assumed that the one thus set apart was responsible for what took place and the others were there to look on and criticise.

In any case what I wish most emphatically to disclaim is that I have been the "medium" when eleven or nineteen other persons were present. It may be right to credit me with a twelfth or twentieth part but not more unless some of the others were unsuitable and a greater share of the responsibility thereby fell on one or more of the other members of the circle.

If these conclusions—the result of many years work and bitter experience—are accepted and followed by investigators and circle-holders in the future, then it is well that we have tried different methods and found which were faulty. I do not however think we have yet found or tried the best method of pursuing this investigation. Others who take up the work where I have laid it down may find safer and better roads than I have trodden. There is so much to learn, so much to understand. Even at the best we but "See through a glass darkly" and grope our way in the darkness. Still, steering our course by the light which shines fitfully through the shadows we may yet reach that fuller light in which "We may know even as we also are known."

Now my task is done. They who come after me may perchance suffer as I have suffered, through ignorance of God's laws. Yet the world is wiser than it was, and it may be that they who take up the work in the next generation will not have to fight, as I did, the narrow bigotry and harsh judgements of the "unco' guid." Still I will not wish them too smooth a road, for it seems to me that, looking backward, I find the troubles that have attended my search—and they have been many—sink into insignificance. Nor do I regret them. They have been the monitors warning me that I had wandered from the right road, and though I knew it not, at the time, were my best friends. Now at last I have found what I have been seeking through these long years; years of hard work interspersed with sunshine and storms, with pleasure and pain; now I can cry aloud in jubilant voice to all who will hear: "I have found the truth—and the same great prize may be yours too, if you will seek it honestly, earnestly, humbly, diligently."

THE END.

Printed in Great Britain
by Amazon